50 ideas

you really need to know

religion

Peter Stanford

Quercus

Contents

Introduction

Everyone has an opinion about religion. It may be positive; it may be negative, but it is rarely neutral. The German philosopher Friedrich Nietzsche, who announced confidently in the 1880s that God was dead, would be surprised to see, 120 years after he wrote its obituary, that religion is still a vibrant and widely debated presence on the world stage.

This book is an attempt to go back to basics and present a balanced picture of what religion is and isn't, from its origins, through its history and its highs and lows, to what it stands for in the modern world. Polemicists such as Richard Dawkins, whose 2007 book *The God Delusion* has done so much to feed and embolden anti-religious prejudice, argue that no one can ever present a wholly objective picture of religion. He may well be right, but it has been my constant endeavour throughout what follows to leave my own feelings and denominational attachment to one side so as to present as rounded a picture as possible.

If there is one point about religion that needs to be made over and above all others it is that its various manifestations around the globe have much more in common with each other than they have that divides them. I have started and ended this book by focusing on that shared ground. In between these opening and closing reflections are sections chronicling the range of religions around the world. Each faith is explored in a broadly similar fashion, by following its history and development, and setting out the essentials of what it teaches and how that translates into everyday life. I hope that what follows will be an intriguing voyage of discovery, whether you know nothing of religion or whether you have already explored some of the areas covered and put down roots in one (or even several) of them.

Greater knowledge of this major force that continues to shape our world may also provide the chance to move beyond the stereotypes that dog discussion about religion. My aim is not that you arrive at the end of this journey converted, but simply that you feel better equipped to participate in that ongoing debate.

Peter Stanford

01 The God-shaped hole

It is the seventeenth-century French philosopher Blaise Pascal who is usually credited with coining the phrase 'a God-shaped hole' to describe the spiritual vacuum inside every human being that yearns to be filled. The concept, however, goes back much further – to the very origins of life on this planet. For many people argue that the religious impulse, a deep-seated need to find a more profound meaning to existence, went hand in hand with the birth of humankind.

Sincere religious believers, of course, hold that it was God who came first, creating men and women to populate the Earth. 'In the beginning was the Word and the Word was with God and the Word was God' starts John's gospel in the New Testament, while the Upanishads, the sacred texts of Hinduism, claim that the Hiranyagarbha, or golden womb, contained the origins of the universe, and of Brahma, the Hindu god of creation.

> **You have made us for yourself, O Lord, and our heart is restless until it rests in you.**
>
> **St Augustine, 354–430**

Others, though, suggest that the process happened the other way round. There have been many theories about the origin of religion. What all of them accept is that human beings have always created gods. So when the first men and women found themselves confronted by the randomness of their fate – with sickness and suffering just as likely to afflict them as joy and good health – they searched for and

timeline

2 million years ago

First humans and birth of the cult of the Sky god

discovered an explanation for these otherwise inexplicable turns of fortune by attributing them to the actions of a distant deity.

A more precise starting point for the idea of a man-made God is found 14,000 years ago in the Middle East, where historians and archaeologists have detected evidence that the forces of nature – the wind, the sun, the stars – as well as less tangible but nonetheless keenly felt entities or spirits believed to exist in the landscape, were personalized and worshipped as gods with human characteristics.

A subsequent stage in this process occurred in the centuries between 800 and 300 BCE, known to history as the Axial Age. During this period, the search for meaning in life turned on figures such as Buddha, Socrates, Confucius and Jeremiah, who all shared a view that there was a transcendent or spiritual dimension to existence, and who tried for the first time to formulate that idea. The primitive notion of a deity grew more distinct and refined.

These attempts to define divine overlordship eventually resulted in

The origin of the idea of god

Many historians and theologians have sought to prove that the concept of God originated in the human mind. One of the most influential writers on the subject was the German anthropologist, ethnologist and Catholic priest, Wilhelm Schmidt (1868–1954), whose twelve-volume *The Origin of the Idea of God* was first published in 1912. His theory of 'primitive monotheism' held that at the dawn of humankind, man fashioned a benevolent creator god – often referred to as the 'Sky god', since he was thought to reside above the Earth in a region that came to be known as the heavens – to provide an explanation for the otherwise inexplicable things, both good and bad, that happened on Earth. This god was so remote from the dilemmas of human life that it seemed pointless to make images of him, or to worship him in rituals led by holy men and women. Alienated by this sensation of distance, people turned instead to more approachable deities, shaped in the image and likeness of humans. According to Schmidt, the cult of the Sky god persisted only among isolated peoples, such as some African and Latin American tribes, and the Aborigines of Australia.

14,000 BCE

Origins of monotheism

800–300 BCE

Axial Age

the various denominations and faiths that are part of the religious world today. While they all still share the common ground of addressing ethical behaviour and the question of how individuals should relate to each other, they differ in how this should be done – in other words, what might loosely be termed doctrine. For instance, Christianity, Judaism and Islam are monotheistic religions. This means that they believe in a single all-powerful god. Hinduism and other Eastern faiths, by contrast, have a pantheon of gods.

❛If I knew him, I would be him.❜

Rabbi Joseph Albo, 1380–1445

Shadowy figures With the Axial Age came the writing down in holy books of the various religious traditions, an accompanying growth in theological study, and the establishment of codes of behaviour governing membership of a particular faith. Yet to this day, in most faiths the exact nature of the deity remains shadowy. Sometimes, as in Taoism and Confucianism, this is deliberate, to place the emphasis on living an ethical life of faith rather than placing a premium on theological speculation. Yet often it is accepted that the deity is beyond conventional words. The *Penny Catechism* of the Catholic Church, a popular digest of that denomination's essential rules and beliefs, and widely used until the 1960s, consisted of a series of questions and answers. To the enquiry 'What is God?', it replied opaquely: 'God is the Supreme Spirit, Who alone exists of Himself, and is infinite in all perfections.'

Any definition of the divine remains cloaked in abstractions and taboos. Jews are forbidden to pronounce the sacred name of God, and Muslims may not depict the divine in visual imagery. Yet that very mystery seems only to heighten the appeal of religion as a way of bringing order to an otherwise unpredictable world.

An ever-changing deity Human needs and desires have changed as the world evolves, and continue to change as the planet and its population face new challenges. Concepts of the divine also evolve and change, though most religions prefer not to acknowledge this, presenting themselves instead as unwavering both in the essentials of their faith, and in the rules that shape its practice within institutions.

Hard-wired for god?

Some scientists have recently produced research to show that the human brain is predisposed or hard-wired for belief in God. According to British academics at Bristol University, human beings are programmed to believe in God because it gives them a better chance of survival. A 2009 study by Bruce Hood, professor of developmental psychology, into the way children's brains develop suggests that during the process of evolution, those people with religious tendencies began to benefit from their beliefs – possibly by working in groups to ensure the future of their community. As a consequence, 'supernatural beliefs' became hard-wired into our brains from birth, leaving us receptive to the claims of religious organizations. Professor Hood's research shows that 'children have a natural, intuitive way of reasoning that leads them to all kinds of supernatural beliefs about how the world works. As they grow up they overlay these beliefs with more rational approaches, but the tendency to illogical supernatural beliefs remains as religion.' These conclusions echo other findings – notably by a group at the Centre for the Science of the Mind at Oxford University, published in 2008 – which have uncovered evidence linking religious feelings to particular parts of the brain. Devout Catholics shown a picture of the Virgin Mary experienced less pain when given an electric shock than non-believers because they underwent a greater degree of deadening activity in the right ventrolateral frontal cortex area of the brain.

So the idea of a deity remains remarkably flexible, and it is this flexibility, according to some people, that has enabled the concept to survive for so long. This suggestion implies a degree of calculation by religious leaders – that they have tailored their presentation to satisfy the particular needs of specific periods. That God is ultimately unknowable, however, is spelt out explicitly by all the faiths, which teach that it is in the quest to know God, or the gods, that we seek and hopefully find value and meaning in life.

the condensed idea
Deities explain the inexplicable

02 Sacred texts

In the process of shaping the concept of a deity as the explanation for the otherwise inexplicable swings between joy and torment in individual lives, religions have distilled what was often originally an oral tradition into sacred texts that have come to represent a thread of continuity and timeless wisdom for believers through the ages.

In all written material there is a relationship between the reader and the word on the page, but for religious believers, their sacred texts take that relationship to new heights. Some will speak of their holy book falling open in front of them on a page that provides a clear answer to the precise dilemma they are currently confronting. Others use their daily reading of religious texts to provide them with guidance in their everyday lives. In all sorts of ways religious texts are invested with faith, and become a practical, spiritual and moral yardstick, the ultimate authority in judging behaviour. Below, we discuss three of the best-known sacred works; others are dealt with later in the book.

The Bible The Bible, the holy book of Christians, is divided into two sections, the Old and the New Testaments. The former, which was written between approximately 1200 BCE and 200 BCE, begins with the creation of the world, and though it contains prophecies of a Messiah who is yet to come, it ends before the birth of Jesus. The latter, dating from 40 CE to 160 CE, covers the life, teachings, death and resurrection of Jesus, and ends (in most versions) with a glimpse of the end of the world and the final judgement. It is estimated that six billion copies of the Bible have been sold in the last two hundred years alone.

timeline

*c.*700 BCE	*c.*586 BCE
First of 13 Hindu Upanishads written	Jews' exile from Jerusalem prompts the Torah

Some Christians insist that the account of the creation of the world given in the Book of Genesis at the start of the Old Testament is literally true – that God created the Earth in six days and rested on the seventh. Others accept that this flies in the face of scientific knowledge. Throughout the Bible there are many conflicting details and statements, but most Christians prefer to believe that despite the contradictions, the Bible possesses an essential truth. For some, especially in the Protestant tradition, it is the supreme arbiter in matters of religion.

Are the gospels true?

The four gospels (a word meaning 'good news') collected in the New Testament of the Bible are for Christians the key accounts of the life of Jesus. Yet none of them is a first-hand narrative. They are not, to take the word as it is typically understood today, gospel – that is, infallibly true in every respect. For a start, they were written decades after Jesus's death, with the oldest existing manuscript versions dating from only the third century. Moreover, they all offer different – often strikingly so – accounts of the basic details of Jesus's life.

Most Christians believe that the gospels are the result of a complex process of authorship that makes them much more than straightforward historical chronicles. They are part reportage, part the setting down in writing of existing oral traditions stretching back to when Jesus was alive, part preaching, part reference back to Old Testament prophecies, part commentary on political events at the time of writing, and part works of literature and imagination. The exact proportions of each element are hotly disputed.

> **The Bible's authority for Christians lies in the fact they have a special relationship with it that can never be altered, like the relationship of parent and child.**
> Diarmaid MacCulloch, Professor of the History of the Church, University of Oxford, 2009

*c.*100 BCE	*c.*CE 40	*c.*CE 635
Buddhist scriptures recorded	St Paul writes earliest sections of the New Testament	Qur'an started after death of Muhammad

The Torah The term Torah can refer to the Hebrew Bible (which overlaps with the Old Testament but does not mirror it), along with the rabbinic teachings that evolved during the first six centuries CE. It is, however, more often used to describe the first five books of the Bible – Genesis, Exodus, Leviticus, Numbers and Deuteronomy, the 'books of Moses'. Jews believe that God dictated the Torah to Moses on Mount Sinai fifty days after their exodus from Egyptian slavery – though this can only be true of certain sections of the five books, sometimes referred to as the 'Oral Torah'. They believe that the Torah shows how God wants them to live – as laid down in 613 commandments. Another factor that binds the five books together is that they are all about God's concern for his 'chosen' people of Israel.

The Torah scroll is regarded as the most sacred object in a Jewish synagogue. It is usually kept in an 'ark', or cupboard, and is revealed at the climax of the liturgy, when it is paraded solemnly among the congregation, who show their respect by brushing it with the tassels of their prayer shawls.

Buddha and scripture

The Buddha (Siddhartha Gautama) fought throughout his life against the cult of personality, and tried to direct the attention of his disciples away from himself. His life was not important, he declared. What mattered was the truth he had discovered, which was rooted in the deepest structure of existence – *dharma*, or a fundamental law of life for gods, humans and animals alike. The Buddhist scriptures are therefore unlike other holy books in that they tell us very little about the Buddha himself, to the extent that some Western scholars in the nineteenth century doubted he had ever existed. These scriptures run to many volumes, in various Asian languages, and their authenticity is a matter of much scholarly debate. It is believed that they were not written down until the first century BCE, around 400 years after the Buddha lived.

The Qur'an Muslims believe that the Qur'an was revealed to the Prophet Muhammad bit by bit over a period of 23 years. It consists of the exact words of Allah and so, unlike holy books in other faiths, involves no human authorship. Muhammad's own teachings are contained elsewhere, in the Hadith, which are a series of oral traditions relating to the Prophet's words and deeds. The Qur'an was first set down in writing by Muhammad's secretary and follower Zayd ibn Thabit soon after the Prophet's death in 632. It contains 114 chapters and is not arranged in chronological order. Islam rejects pictorial illustrations, but the decorated writing – or calligraphy – in some ancient copies is amongst the great art treasures of the world.

> **'Let holy reading always be at hand.'**
> **St Jerome, c.410**

There is a precise ritual attached to reading the Qur'an. Muslims must 'prepare the heart' and wash their hands. Women usually cover their heads – as for prayer. There is a special sitting position – disciplined and alert – on the floor, with the Qur'an on a stand or *kursi* in front of the reader.

Though the words of the Qur'an are unchanging, different translations and interpretations place varying emphases on them. In recent times, for example, some Muslims have attempted to justify violent atrocities by reference to jihad – or struggle – a concept they place in a military context, even though Muhammad is not portrayed by Islam as a man of violence.

The significance of all these holy books goes beyond any direct, or indirect, connection to the deity. They are seen as having the power both to encapsulate the hopes of humankind as no other text does, and to speak directly to those aspirations in a way that is unique, tangible and empowering.

the condensed idea
Religions venerate holy books

03 Good and evil

Once the notion of a Sky God had begun to evolve into a deity shaping the world and its destiny from the heavens, the question was asked: why would such a deity allow human beings to suffer? It is a dilemma that religions still struggle to answer to the satisfaction of many. One solution was for religion to shift the blame, so that whatever went wrong in the world, and in individual lives, was now the fault of an evil spirit rather than an omnipotent God.

This approach presented Earth as the apocalyptic battleground for a cosmic clash between good gods and malign deities, with humankind as cannon fodder. There is early evidence of a belief in an evil horned spirit, half man, half beast, in cave paintings found at the Caverne des Trois Frères at Ariège in France that date back 9,000 years. The pantheon of the ancient Egyptians from the fourth century BCE featured a series of two-faced deities, one profile benign, the other menacing, the most prominent of which combined Horus, the hawk-headed Sky god, and Seth, depicted as a snake or pig and representing evil. In Egyptian holy legend the two are locked in an eternal mortal combat.

The hostile spirit The high point of this belief in equal and opposite divine forces competing for world domination occurred in the twelfth century BCE in ancient Persia. The sacred texts of Zoroastrianism, the Gathas, tell the story of the power struggle between the good god Ahura Mazda, lord of wisdom and justice, and the hostile spirit Angra Mainyu, who had invaded the world and filled it with violence, falsehood, dust, dirt, disease, death and decay. Good was

timeline

c.1200 BCE
Zoroaster's apocalyptic vision

c.585 BCE
Jews in Babylon encounter Zoroastrianism

Zoroastrianism

There are an estimated 479,000 Zoroastrians in the world today, many of them in India among the Parsi people. However, Zoroastrianism's greatest influence arguably lies in the role it played in the development of other religions, which borrowed and adapted the insights of its founder. Zoroaster, who is thought to have lived around 1200 BCE, was troubled by the suffering of his own people in what is now Iraq and Iran. In the Gathas, seventeen hymns attributed to him, he ponders on humanity's vulnerability and impotence. These he ascribes not just to a creator god, but also to his opposite and equal – 'two primal spirits, twins destined to be in conflict' with each other. He is thought to have been the first to introduce such an apocalyptic vision to religion.

separated from evil, the pure from the impure. This concept of opposing divine principles is known as dualism, and has over time been flirted with by many religions.

During the Jewish exile to Babylon in the sixth century BCE, for example, the notion of Zoroastrian dualism became so familiar to the Jews that when they came to reflect on their defeat by the Babylonian forces, and the destruction of the Temple in Jerusalem, some of them decided that such a failure was caused not by Yahweh, but rather by the intrusion of an evil spirit that had come between the Israelites and their God.

❝Sine diabolo, nullus dominus.❞

('Without the Devil, no God.') Traditional saying

C.CE 30
Jesus battles with Devil in gospels

C.CE 1200
Christian inquisition seeks out devil-worshippers

The face of evil Dualism, in turn, was passed on to Christianity. There is one prominent strand in the New Testament that presents human existence in terms of a clash between Jesus and the Devil – notably during Jesus's 40 days and 40 nights in the desert wilderness, when he is tempted by the Devil with all the riches of the world. Later in the New Testament, in the Book of Revelation, there is an account of the end of time, when the Devil and his supporters are finally defeated by God but are left to prey on suggestible human beings until the final day of judgement dawns, thereby polluting the Earth with sin and suffering.

Exorcism

Although the Devil has been downgraded from the role he was given by the medieval Catholic Church, the practice of exorcism still survives. The Vatican maintains a network of priest exorcists around the globe, and continues to believe that in rare cases, humans can suffer demonic possession. In March 1982, it was reported by the prefect of the papal household, Cardinal Jacques Martin, that Pope John Paul II had personally exorcised a young woman believed to be possessed by the Devil. The rites of exorcism used by the Catholic Church are based on Jesus's actions in casting out demons in the gospels. The ritual remains largely unchanged from that set out in 1614, and incorporates prayers, the laying on of hands, making the sign of the cross and sprinkling with holy water. There are also minor rites of exorcism in the wording of the baptismal service, and when a priest blesses a new home.

Although Christianity is officially monotheist – believing in one God as the source of everything in the world – in practice it has for long periods tempered this theory with a limited dose of dualism. By contrast, both Judaism and Islam are more purist in their monotheism. Though there are minor Devil-like figures in the Qur'an, called Shaytan and Iblis, they are largely impotent. 'I have no authority over you,' Shaytan says, 'except

> **❝He is the weak place of popular religion, the vulnerable belly of the crocodile.❞**
>
> **Percy Bysshe Shelley on the Devil, 1821**

that I called you and you obeyed. Do not therefore blame me, but blame yourselves.' Judaism, meanwhile, prefers to talk not of evil spirits but of an evil inclination – the *yetzer hara* – in each and every person.

It was Christianity that portrayed the Devil as the face of evil. Throughout the medieval period the Church taught that the Devil waited at every turn to woo the faithful away from God and the path of righteousness, and into sin and ultimately damnation in hell. Even the Protestant reformers embraced this view. Martin Luther was so convinced of the reality of the Devil that he believed his own bowel problems were caused by demonic possession.

In more recent times, mainstream Christianity has spoken with reluctance on the subject of evil. However, the figure of the Devil remains popular in more evangelical Christian churches, where weakness or illness is still sometimes believed to be the result of giving in to him. Exorcism ceremonies are held for possessed individuals. More generally, any form of disturbance is attributed to an external reality – that is, the Devil – rather than to internal psychological, sociological or emotional factors in a person's life. The Devil may have been sidelined by the established Church, but the concept of opposing divine principles remains a powerful one among many believers.

the condensed idea
Good and evil are at war in us

04 Life and death

Religion aims not only to inspire moral and ethical standards in this world; it also holds up the promise of life after death. This might be in a celestial paradise such as the Christian heaven or the Muslim *djanna*, or as part of the cycle of death and reincarnation whereby the spirit is reborn in various manifestations, known in the Hindu Upanishads as *samsara*.

All religions incorporate an element of judgement in death, linking conduct on earth with reward or punishment afterwards. This idea dates back to the ancient Egyptians and the civilization that thrived along the Nile and its delta from the fourth millennium BCE until the time of classical Greece and Rome. The Egyptians believed in life after death, as the mummies and artefacts in the death chambers of the pyramids make abundantly clear. In the domain of Osiris, lord of the dead, the *ka* – the intellect and spirit of each individual – would be placed on one side of a set of scales, and an ostrich feather on the other. Goodness was deemed light. If the scales tipped the wrong way, it meant consignment to an underworld of monsters. Verdicts were recorded by Osiris's son, Thoth; this is the origin of the lavishly illustrated Books of the Dead that have survived from ancient Egypt.

Judgement in death Despite the fact that they had been exiled in Egypt, the Israelites did not borrow this notion of judgement in death when they first established their own kingdom in the Holy Land around 1200 BCE. The Hebrew scriptures and the early books of the Old Testament speak of *sheol* as a subterranean resting place to which all

timeline

c.4000 BCE

Ancient Egyptians weigh
the souls of the dead

c.800 BCE

Judaism introduces judgement
into *sheol*, land of the dead

were sent at death, regardless of merit on earth. Only a handful of exceptional individuals, such as the prophet Elijah, are described as going to heaven to join God. However, by around the eighth century BCE, the element of judgement at the end of life was introduced into Judaism, and was then passed to Christianity.

It has traditionally been taught by Christians that those who follow Jesus's teachings will go to heaven for eternity, while those who reject them will suffer torment in hell. Somewhere between the two is purgatory – a waiting room for heaven – first mentioned in theological discussions around 1170 and referred to explicitly by a pope in 1254. It is closely linked to 2 November, All Souls' Day in the Christian calendar, when believers pray that dead friends and relatives will be ushered from purgatory into the final joy of heaven.

Final enlightenment The Upanishads, the key documents of Hinduism, written between 700 and 300 BCE, are quite specific in their descriptions of *samsara*. If you have stolen grain in one life, you will be a rat in the next. If you kill a priest, you will be reborn as a pig. Hindus believe that *moksha* – the liberation of the soul from the oppression of the body, which leads

A Hindu heaven

Though Hinduism generally avoids detailed portrayals of the afterlife, there is in the Kausitaki Upanishad a description of the landscape where those who have emerged from *samsara* enjoy union with the infinite spirit, Brahman. 'He first arrives at the lake Ara. He crosses it with his mind, but those who go into it without complete knowledge drown in it. Then he arrives near the watchmen, Muhurta, but they flee from him. Then he arrives at the river Vijara, which he crosses with just his mind. There he shakes off his good and bad deeds, which fall upon his relatives – the good deeds upon the ones he likes and the bad deeds upon the ones he dislikes ... Freed from his good and bad deeds, this man, who has knowledge of Brahman, goes on to Brahman.'

*c.*700–300 BCE
Upanishads describe *samsara*

1321 BCE
Dante's Paradiso

> **A thing too stupendous for the tongue to tell of or the imagination to picture.**
>
> **As-Suyati, 1445–1505, on djanna**

to final enlightenment – is a long process. At the end of it will be found not so much a place as a state of mind, described in the Upanishads as self-abandonment.

While reincarnation is sometimes regarded by Western Christians as an attractive possibility compared with the finality of death, for Hindus the cycle of *samsara* is not just an opportunity to grow spiritually, but also punishment, because it signifies that the believer has not yet achieved final enlightenment.

Garden paradise   In many religious traditions, the exact nature of the afterlife remains unclear. Eastern religions say almost nothing about it, though Shinto and Taoism include elements of ancestor worship. Islam teaches that *djanna* is a garden paradise where, according to the Qur'an, a banquet of the finest foods is waiting, but further theological

Cockaigne

Medieval Western travellers to Islamic lands reported back that the Qur'an promised Muslim martyrs that they would be greeted in *djanna* by beautiful virgins. While the Qu'ran itself is unclear on this – depending on which translation you prefer, the exact description can refer to anything from 'companions' to 'full-breasted maidens'. The Hadith, traditional sayings traced with varying degrees of credibility to Muhammad, includes (again in some versions) the promise: 'The least [reward] for the people of Heaven is 80,000 servants and 72 wives, over which stands a dome of pearls, aquamarine and ruby.' Such texts encouraged exaggerations in Western literature of the period about the eroticism of *djanna* that have persisted to this day. Thus the *Liber Scalae* or *Book of the Ladder* of 1264 described *djanna* as a place with ruby-encrusted walls where virgins lay waiting to pleasure newcomers in pavilions of emeralds and pearls, set amid fruit trees and tables laden with food and drink. Descriptions such as these are believed in their turn to have been the inspiration for the fantasy land of Cockaigne, an earthbound paradise of plenty, recorded in many medieval European texts and illustrations.

> **The Way of Heaven has no favourites.**
> **It is always with the good man.**
>
> **Lao-Tzu, 6th century BCE**

speculation about what is an otherwise abstract idea is dismissed as *zannah,* or self-indulgent whimsy. In the fifth century, St Augustine, arguably the most influential writer and thinker in Christian history, insisted that heaven was simply ineffable – beyond words.

Despite this coalition of powerful voices warning against attempts to imagine the afterlife, it is a concept that has intrigued and inspired a long line of theologians, mystics, artists and writers. The fourteenth-century Italian poet Dante memorably mapped out Paradiso as part of his *Divine Comedy*, though even he shied away from describing the inner core of heaven. Dante's depiction of hell – or Inferno – as a series of layers descending into the Earth is one shared with Jainism, the ancient Indian religion, which sees itself as operating within a universe with two levels of heaven above the Earth and two of hell below it.

Several Western artists depicting life after death have borrowed from Virgil, the first-century BCE Roman poet, the image of the Elysian Fields, entered symbolically through a gate. And medieval Christian mystics, many of them virginal nuns, favoured the image of Christ waiting for the souls of the faithful departed to arrive in heaven as a bridegroom would wait for his bride.

As we can see, therefore, in the many and varied attempts to imagine life after death, there are two distinct schools – one that envisages it as a cleaned-up version of Earth, and the other that, in line with Augustine, insists that in order to satisfy souls for eternity, it must be beyond our imagination and therefore can only be described in metaphor.

the condensed idea
Death is not the end

05 The Golden Rule

At the moral core of all religions lies a simple shared imperative, often referred to as 'the Golden Rule'. The exact wording of this rule differs from one religion to another, but the essential meaning is the same, and is best summed up in Western societies by the familiar command: 'Never do to others what you wouldn't want them to do to you.'

Confucians know this code of behaviour as *shu* – consideration – in the sense that you show consideration for others because you can't separate out your own pain, or hope, or satisfaction from that of other people. Buddhists talk of a lifelong approach to the issue, and their rule is summed up in a phrase of the Buddha's from one of the Buddhist scriptures, *Samyutta Nikaya* (literally 'kindred sayings'): 'A person who loves the self should not harm the self of others.' In Christianity, in similar fashion, Jesus tells his followers in Matthew's gospel, 'So always treat others as you would like them to treat you. That is the meaning of the Law and the Prophets.' It might justifiably be added that this is the meaning of the New Testament too.

By contrast, Jews explain the rule in the form of a story. The celebrated scholar Rabbi Hillel (80 BCE–CE 30) is approached by a pagan who promises to convert to Judaism if Hillel can teach him Torah while standing on one leg. 'What is hateful to yourself, do not to your fellow

timeline

*c.*530 BCE	*c.*480 BCE
Confucius first states Golden Rule	Buddha urges love of others not self

The first formulator of the Golden Rule

Confucius, in the sixth century BCE, was arguably the first religious leader to articulate the Golden Rule. It sprang from his core belief that holiness was inseparable from altruism; that everything always came back to treating others with respect. 'Our master's way,' said one of his disciples, 'is nothing but this: doing-your-best-for-others [known to Confucians as *zhong*] and consideration [*shu*].' Confucius developed many of his insights in conversation with the group of followers he gathered around him. In the *Analects*, the main source for accounts of his life and teaching, he is constantly debating with them. 'Is there,' asks Zigong, one of the group, 'any single saying that one can act upon each and every day?' Confucius replies: 'Perhaps the saying about consideration.'

man,' replies the rabbi, perched on one foot. 'That is the whole of the Torah and the remainder is but commentary. Go learn it.'

A shared ideal There are, of course, contrary forces within the religious traditions. The books of the Old Testament that are sacred to both Jews and Christians tell of Yahweh commanding the Israelites to drive out other inhabitants of the Promised Land by the sword, and

> **❝Never impose on others what you would not choose for yourself.❞**
>
> **Confucius, 551–479 BCE**

C.CE 30

Rabbi Hillel defines Golden Rule

C.CE 60

Golden Rule included in gospels

Rabbi Hillel and the Golden Rule

The Christian Bible presents the Pharisees in an unfavourable light during the events surrounding Jesus's crucifixion, but history indicates that they were in fact the most progressive and inclusive force within Judaism in the first century CE, a time when the Jewish homeland was occupied by the Romans, who put down a rebellion with great brutality and destroyed the Temple in Jerusalem. Rabbi Hillel was one of the leading Pharisee teachers. He held that God could be experienced everywhere and by everyone, not just by a privileged elite through elaborate rituals in the Temple. Charity, he

believed, was the most important human endeavour, hence his championing of the Golden Rule. For him it was the spirit of Jewish law that mattered, not the letter. This was conveyed in another Talmudic story, in which two Jews are surveying the ruins of the Temple. 'Woe is it that the place, where the sins of Israel find atonement, is laid to waste,' says one. 'Grieve not,' replies the other, 'we have an atonement equal to the Temple, the doing of loving deeds.'

even permitting the rape and murder of their womenfolk. But if it is possible to identify a single thread linking all religions, it is their mutual attachment to the Golden Rule.

The power of the rule lies in the fact that it contains what is and always has been for human beings a profoundly countercultural and counterintuitive idea – namely, not to put ourselves and our own needs first. However instinctive that impulse may be, all religions teach that it is morally wrong-headed and potentially self-defeating.

> **‘Hurt no one so that no one may hurt you.’**

Muhammad, 632 CE

Religion might be reasonably defined as an attempt to find a way whereby individuals can interact peacefully, societies can operate in a just, inclusive and equitable way, and different societies and tribes can satisfy their own needs while co-existing with others on the same planet. The first principle of these various aims is the Golden Rule.

A radical challenge In many ways the Golden Rule represents a radical notion – that by putting others first, we are not, as is often suggested in Western secular society, showing weakness, but rather moral strength. There is also the suggestion, implicit or explicit, that by treating others well we are ultimately helping ourselves, for if we set standards in our own behaviour, other people will match them in their dealings with us, and as a result everybody benefits.

The Golden Rule also touches on another feature of religion – that faith is about doing rather than simply believing. Showing empathy, concern and compassion, yielding rather than judging: these are the lessons that are emphasized in the sacred scriptures, yet often they become lost behind dogma, doctrine, rules and rituals.

the condensed idea
Do as you would be done by

06 Rites and rituals

All religions have their own ceremonies and rites of passage. The purpose of these is to forge a link between humankind and the gods, to provide a forum for spiritual exploration, and to remind individual believers that they are part of something bigger than themselves, both in their own time and throughout history.

For many believers, the rites and rituals of their faith give shape to their lives. The sacraments of Christianity, for example, celebrate the landmarks of an individual's life from birth through adulthood and on to death. Muslims are required to pray five times a day – the call to prayer being part of *shahadah*, the first of the 'Five Pillars' of Islamic practice. And the Buddha taught 2500 years ago that regular meditation was the pathway to enlightenment. It continues to this day to form the core of the life of a Buddhist.

The various religions, however, have differing approaches to their rites and rituals. Islam, for instance, teaches that any building can be converted into a mosque, and that none of the traditional features of the great mosques are compulsory. . Hindus do gather in temples to worship, but there is no obligation on them ever to do so. Rites can just as well be carried out at home in front of a personal shrine.

Within Christianity, the house-church movement favours simple services, using everyday contemporary language, in believers' own

timeline

*c.*3rd century BCE	CE 70
Earliest synagogues in Egypt	Destruction of Temple in Jerusalem

The Sacraments in Christianity

Many branches of the Christian faith celebrate a series of sacraments that mark the significant events in an individual believer's life. Catholicism, for example, has a lifelong structure of seven sacraments: baptism (formally entering the Church), usually as an infant; reconciliation (once called confession) and holy communion (receiving the bread and wine as the body and blood of Jesus), both around the age of eight; confirmation (making an adult commitment to the faith), in the mid-teens; marriage, as an adult; ordination (becoming a priest), again as an adult; and finally the sacrament of the sick (once extreme unction), usually when death is close.

homes. At the other end of the Christian scale, though, are the elaborate High Church celebrations, held in ancient and ornate buildings, presided over by ministers in dazzling vestments and carried out according to strict patterns and precedents that date back hundreds of years, sometimes even in the 'dead' language of Latin.

Higher symbolism Rites and rituals carry with them a heavy burden of symbolism, part of the attempt by religions to lift the eyes of believers from the everyday and earthbound to the spiritual plain. In medieval Christianity, even the spires and towers of cathedrals were held to be not simply an outward sign of prestige, or a beacon in the landscape for believers, but an almost literal reaching-up to the heavens. And in Taoism, the ancient religious and philosophical tradition that originated in China with Lao-Tzu in the sixth century BCE, purification and meditation rituals of chanting, playing

For where two or three meet in my name, I shall be there with them.
Matthew 18:20

c.7th century CE
Mosques develop from open-air gathering places

1626
St Peter's Basilica in Rome completed

instruments and dancing are often so complex and technical that they are left to the priests, with the congregation playing little part. Because of the significance that is attached to it, there is a danger that ritual can be regarded as an end in itself. Time-honoured words and phrases repeated among fellow believers in a familiar setting often become as treasured as the actual theology or insights of religions. Guru Nanak, the founder in sixteenth-century India of Sikhism, warned specifically against thinking that God could only be approached through ritual. Spending time in prayer should be likened to spending time in the company of a friend, he said. Unlike members of some other religions, Sikhs therefore worship God in his abstract form, without using images or statues to help them. They do, however, gather for communal worship in *gurdwaras*, or temples.

The rites of Hajj in Islam

It is compulsory for every Muslim who can afford it, and who is well enough, to make the pilgrimage once in their lifetime to Mecca, the mother-town of Islam. This is known as the Hajj – literally 'to set out with a definite purpose'. There are four parts to the ritual of the Hajj: (1) Ihram – to wear special clothing and to enter into a spiritual or holy state of mind; (2) Tawaf – to circle seven times, in an anticlockwise direction, the Ka'bah, the cube-shaped shrine in Mecca, and, if possible, to touch the black stone it contains (al-Hajar al-Aswad), which is said to have been sent down from heaven; (3) Wuquf – to go to the plain of Arafat, 24 kilometres east of Mecca, and pray before Allah on or near the Mount of Mercy; and (4) on returning from Arafat, to circle the Ka'bah again. Only then can a pilgrim claim the title *hajji* for men or *hajjah* for women.

All faiths emphasize the fact that ritual provides a link between the spiritual and material domains. In the Taoist ceremony of *chiao* (or *jiao*), which concentrates on cosmic renewal, each household in a village brings an offering for the local deities. A priest then dedicates the offerings in the names of the donor families, performs a ritual to restore order to the universe, and also asks the gods to bring peace and prosperity to the village.

Because of their symbolism, and the faith invested in them by believers, religious rituals have changed very little over the centuries. This is largely by design, since it allows contemporary believers in a rapidly changing world to experience the sense of walking in the footsteps of earlier generations who shared their faith. Christians, for example, when they recite the Lord's Prayer, are using words written in the gospels 2,000 years ago, although today they usually do so in their own language.

Despite the many differences between them, there are also overlaps and interchanges in the rites and rituals of the various faiths. This is sometimes a result of the fact that they have a common origin, but it can be more calculating. When Christianity began to replace paganism across great swathes of Europe in the first millennium CE, it consciously adapted elements of pagan rituals, by marking the feasts of Christ's birth and death at the pagan winter solstice and spring equinox respectively.

Saying and meaning There is a teaching element to religious rites and rituals. Reading aloud from sacred books, a practice that dates from an age where the majority of the congregation were illiterate, helps believers to focus on the essence of their faith. Muslims are encouraged to learn passages from the Qur'an by heart from an early age so that they can recite them without reference to the text. And as Christians intone the Nicene Creed, or Credo, they repeat and absorb a compressed version of the key doctrines of their Church. Historically this process was known in Christianity by the Latin phrase *lex orandi, lex credendi*, which translates as 'the law of prayer is the law of belief'. Put more simply, what you say out loud in a rite or ritual is what you come to believe in your heart.

> 'You can set up an altar to God in your mind by means of prayer.'
>
> St John Chrysostom, c.390

the condensed idea
Private faith has a public dimension

07 The life of Christ

The four gospels collected in the New Testament of the Bible tell the story of the Jewish carpenter's son in first-century Palestine who was crucified but miraculously rose again from the dead. These accounts of the actions and teachings of Jesus Christ are the rock on which Christianity is built, and they continue to inform the lives of an estimated 2.1 billion Christians around the globe; in other words, just under one in three of the world's population.

Christianity teaches that Jesus was the son of God, made human in order to redeem the sins of the world. Two of the gospel writers, Mark and John, begin their accounts with Jesus already an adult and being baptized by his cousin, John. The other two, Matthew and Luke, instead start with the familiar tale, recalled by Christians each Christmas, of Jesus's mother, Mary, and her virgin birth (her husband Joseph, the carpenter, was not Jesus's real father), and of the child being visited in a Bethlehem stable by shepherds and three kings from the East guided to the place by a star.

The main focus of all four of the gospels, though, is the last three years of the 33 that Christians believe Jesus spent on earth. During this time he left his home in Nazareth and travelled around what is today known as the Holy Land, preaching initially in synagogues and later at vast open-air gatherings. In the process he assembled a core group of 12 male apostles, led by a fisherman, Simon, whom he renamed Peter, as well as a wider crowd of disciples.

timeline

CE 1

Jesus born in Bethlehem

CE 30

Begins public ministry

The four gospels

Although they overlap on a number of events, each of the four gospels contains details not found in any other, and each has its own distinctive style. Mark's is the shortest; it presents Jesus as a man of action and is written with little linguistic ornament. It is also believed to be the earliest of the four, dated around CE 70. Matthew's, by contrast, written towards the end of the first century, gives more space to explaining the actions that are merely catalogued in Mark. It was intended primarily for a Jewish audience and links Jesus back to the prophets, kings and patriarchs of Israel. Luke's gospel is the longest of the four and is poetic in tone. It contains many more stories and images and was written, it is believed, around the end of the first and start of the second century. John's text contains entire sections unlike anything found in the other three; lengthy passages in which Jesus tries to explain who he is and why he has come into the world. It may have been the work of several authors, and has been dated between 100 and 125 CE.

Parables and miracles In the gospels, Jesus favours two main teaching methods – parables and miracles. His parables are memorable stories drawing on an everyday agricultural life that would be familiar to his audience, but also containing a broader moral point. It was a way of getting his message across to a population that was largely uneducated and therefore unlikely to respond to theological abstractions.

> **Apart from Christ we know neither what our life nor our death is.**
>
> **Blaise Pascal, 1662**

CE 33
Put to death

CE 70
First of four gospels written

Jesus's miracles – curing the sick and dying, and in at least two cases bringing the dead back to life, as well as walking on water, casting out demons, and making a few loaves and fishes feed a crowd of five thousand – demonstrated that he had powers greater than that of any mere man, and thus were the tangible proof for those who witnessed them that he was indeed the son of God. They recall the many stories in the Old Testament – known to Jews as the Hebrew scriptures – of miraculous cures brought about by divine intervention.

Sermon on the Mount Jesus's exact message to believers is much debated among the various branches of the Christian family. Its central features, however, are beyond dispute. In his parables, he describes how the world should be; the loving, sharing, caring, compassionate values it should embrace, rather than those it actually does. He talks about these values many times, most notably in the Sermon on the Mount,

Independent evidence of Jesus

Aside from the gospels, there are three other independent historical sources that mention Jesus's life and death. At the end of the first century CE and the beginning of the second, two Roman historians, Tacitus and Pliny, and the Jewish chronicler Josephus all described him as a religious teacher living in Palestine. Tacitus includes the following just after an account of the great fire in Rome that occurred during Emperor Nero's reign in CE 64: 'Nero fastened the guilt of starting the blaze and inflicted the most exquisite tortures on a class hated for their abominations, called Christians by the populace. Christus, from whom the name had its origin, suffered the extreme penalty during the reign of Tiberius [CE 14–37] at the hands of one of our procurators, Pontius Pilatus.'

> **There is in every miracle a silent chiding of the world.**
>
> **John Donne, 1649**

an episode that takes up three of the 28 chapters of Matthew's gospel. This sermon includes the words of the Lord's Prayer, repeated regularly by all Christians, plus Jesus's version of the Golden Rule of treating others as you would want to be treated, his instruction 'do not judge and you will not be judged', and the Beatitudes, which begin: 'Happy are the poor in spirit; theirs is the kingdom of heaven.' With these words, Jesus is identifying himself explicitly with the marginalized and the dispossessed, an impression reinforced later in the gospels when he tells a rich young man to 'go and sell what you own and give the money to the poor, and you will have treasure in heaven'.

Passion and death Jesus's teachings, and his increasing popularity, worried many in the Jewish establishment at the time. They saw him as a threat to their own authority, and so they conspired with the Roman colonial powers to have him put to death. The last week of his life, according to the gospels, was spent in Jerusalem. It began triumphantly, with people welcoming him into the city as the saviour of Israel from foreign domination, but ended with his trial and his death by crucifixion – an ordeal collectively known to Christians as his Passion.

The gospels tell that three days after his death, on Easter Sunday, Jesus rose from the dead. By his death and resurrection he had, it is taught, redeemed the sins of humankind, and after entrusting his mission on Earth to his apostles, who were to become the first leaders of the Christian Church, he ascended into heaven in glory to rejoin his father.

the condensed idea
Jesus Christ is the son of God

08 God and Mammon

Despite the fact that Jesus stressed repeatedly in his teachings his concern for the poor, the marginalized and the dispossessed, the Christian Church, founded in his name, went on to become one of the richest and most powerful institutions the world has ever known. In many ways it can be regarded as the original multinational. Throughout the history of Christianity, the relationship between God and Mammon – a word used in the Bible and taken from the Hebrew for 'money' – has been a troubled one.

In the early years of its existence, the Christian Church survived on the margins of society, often in underground cells, suffering sustained and bloody persecution, most notably at the hands of the Roman Empire. It had only a rudimentary structure and scarce resources. In 312, however, Christianity received formal approval from the Roman Emperor Constantine and became the official religion of empire. With this recognition came access to substantial funds, which prompted a great burst of church-building in Rome and beyond.

In the fourth and fifth centuries, the western part of the Roman Empire slowly crumbled. In the chaos that ensued, the Christian Church managed to retain and indeed expand its power and influence, taking on the mantle of temporal as well as spiritual authority. Under skilled

timeline

CE 64	312
St Peter, the first pope, executed by Romans	Church makes peace with Romans

and ambitious leaders such as Pope Gregory the Great at the end of the sixth century, it successfully converted to Christianity many of the pagans who had been instrumental in destroying the old empire, thus laying the basis for a whole new political set-up, with the Church at its heart. By 800, Charlemagne, King of the Franks, had established his rule over western Europe, and on Christmas Day of that year, he came to Rome and knelt before Pope Leo III to be crowned Holy Roman Emperor. The role of the Christian Church at the heart of world affairs was unmistakable.

> **The Pope! How many divisions has he got?**
>
> Joseph Stalin, 1935

The sale of indulgences

In 1517, Pope Leo X offered indulgences (pardons for sinful behaviour) to Christians who made donations towards the elaborate rebuilding of St Peter's Basilica in Rome. The aggressive selling of these pardons so infuriated Martin Luther (1483–1546), an Augustinian monk and teacher, that he included an attack on the practice in his Ninety-Five Theses, a programme for reform that, according to legend, he nailed to the door of the castle church in Wittenberg in October 1517. In Thesis 28, Luther objected to a particular phrase used in the sale of these indulgences: 'As soon as a coin in the coffer rings, a soul from purgatory springs.' The only thing indulgences guaranteed, countered Luther, was an increase in profit and greed, because pardon was in God's power alone.

800	1517	1787
Pope crowns Charlemagne	Luther rejects sale of indulgences	US constitution separates Church and state

Since then, there have been many high and low points in the relationship between Church and state, but throughout it all, Christianity has continued to play an accepted and sometimes officially recognized role in secular affairs. One consequence of this has been that the Church has amassed great wealth, and under its patronage many extraordinary buildings and works of art have been completed, such as Michelangelo's epic fresco of *The Last Judgement* (1537–41) in the Sistine Chapel, part of the papal palace complex in the Vatican.

Source of dissent The Church's relationship with Mammon has never been a simple one. There has long been a debate about who should have power of patronage in appointing bishops – the local king or ruler, or the Pope in Rome. And it was the practice of selling indulgences to raise cash (see page 33) that alienated the German monk Martin Luther, leading to his break with Catholicism in 1517 and ultimately the Protestant Reformation.

Liberation theology

The idea of liberation theology grew up in Latin America and Asia in the 1960s as both an academic and a practical expression of Catholic Christianity. It urged the Church to follow Jesus's example and make a 'preferential option for the poor'. 'How,' wrote one of its foremost proponents, the Brazilian priest Leonardo Boff, 'are we to be Christians in a world of destruction and injustice? We can be followers of Jesus only by making common cause with the poor and working out the gospel of liberation.' It has proved to be a controversial message. Boff was silenced by the Pope in the 1980s and later left the priesthood. The Catholic leadership in the Vatican fears that liberation theology is too political a gospel and that it risks infecting Christianity with Marxism. In 1986, Pope John Paul II endorsed the ambition to work for the poor, but stressed that it must be done on the basis not of politics but of helping each individual to find a life of freedom from sin.

❝I look upon all the world as my parish.❞

John Wesley, *c.*1780

Today, some countries – such as Britain – still have an established Church that is an acknowledged part of the constitution and a recipient of state funds. However, recent centuries have seen the disestablishment of formal links between Church and state in several hitherto officially Christian countries – notably France – while in others, including the United States, a legal separation of the two is specified in their constitutions. Elsewhere, governments restrict the operation of the Church. In China, for instance, the communist authorities have established a state-run Chinese Catholic Patriotic Association in an effort to replace the 'outside influence' of the Church of Rome on its population.

Spark from heaven The extent of the continuing political influence of Christianity was brought into sharp focus by the papacy of John Paul II (1978–2005). Many people credited him with being the 'spark from heaven' that ignited the revolutions that overthrew communist rule in Eastern Europe from 1989 onwards, including in his native Poland. He is reported to have worked closely with the US administration towards this goal. In other areas, though, John Paul's social and political influence was controversial. For example, his insistence that Church teaching ruled out the use of condoms to help prevent the spread of AIDS was believed by many health-care organizations to have had a powerful impact on government and international community efforts to contain the pandemic, especially in Africa. To this day, the relationship between Church and state continues to cause controversy and debate.

the condensed idea
Religion is political

09 Reformation

For the first thousand years of its existence, the Christian Church lived up to the promise made in the Apostles' Creed, its statement of faith, to be 'one, holy, catholic and apostolic'. Throughout this time, however, there were ongoing tensions between various parts of the Church about doctrine and organization. In the eleventh century came the break between Western and Eastern (Orthodox) Christians. And then, at the start of the sixteenth century, Martin Luther, a German monk, precipitated the Reformation, which has left division in its wake to this day.

By the late fifteenth century, the papacy appeared to be more powerful than ever. The show of wealth, the commissioning of great works of art and the flamboyant lifestyles of some popes suggested an institution in rude health. Beneath this façade, however, Christianity was in moral and spiritual decline. Despairing of the conduct of popes – Alexander VI (1492–1503), for example, was installed while his children from various illicit liaisons looked on unabashed – a series of often small local reform movements began working for spiritual renewal and a return to high moral ideals in the theory and practice of the Church. One such was the Oratory of Divine Love, a charitable institute founded in 1497 in Genoa by Ettore Vernazza, which also became active in Rome, Naples and Bologna. None reached a level where it could effectively challenge the papacy.

Martin Luther When Martin Luther publicly questioned the corruption in the Church in the early years of the sixteenth century, he

timeline

*c.*1490s	1517
Reform-minded brotherhoods founded	Luther nails Ninety-Five Theses to church door

found he was speaking for many disillusioned believers. There was a theological basis to his rebellion, as laid out in the Ninety-Five Theses he famously nailed to the door of a church in Wittenberg in Germany in 1517. He rejected the notion, central to Catholic Christianity then as now, that by doing good deeds you were contributing towards earning yourself a place in heaven after death. Salvation came, he believed, through faith in God. It was not an individual's holiness that counted. It was God's love.

The vernacular Bible

For Luther, the ultimate source of Christian authority was not the say-so of the Pope, or the traditional practice of the Church, but the Bible. In 1521, as the battle raged between the German princes who defended him and the papacy that wanted to silence him, Luther set himself the task of translating the New Testament into German. There had been earlier efforts to make the Bible available in the vernacular – local language – rather than Church Latin. Where Luther's effort stood out was in his scholarship – he returned to the original Greek version to rediscover the Bible's true meaning – and his use of the sort of German spoken by ordinary men and women. He wanted to make the Bible accessible to all. He published his New Testament in 1522, and a full German Bible in 1534. Elsewhere, a Dutch Bible (1526), a French Bible (1528) and a Zurich Bible (1531) were published. These efforts inspired others, and in 1611, the King James' Bible, a translation into English, appeared.

Luther's attack benefited from his skill as a speaker, and from his use of advances in printing techniques to produce books and leaflets to get his message across. He was also helped by Rome's tendency to dismiss him as irrelevant rather than appreciating the fact that he was a formidable

1532
Henry VIII breaks with Rome

1541
Luther rejects compromise at Regentsburg

1545
Council of Trent

opponent who was gaining support. When he was taken up by German princes keen to loosen the papacy's grip on their lands, he realised that he had found powerful political sponsors who enabled him to escape arrest and punishment by the Church, and condemnation by the Holy Roman Emperor, Charles V, at the Diet of Worms in 1521.

Zwingli and Calvin

Ulrich Zwingli (1484–1531) reacted in much the same way to the moral and spiritual decline in Roman Christianity as Luther, but he did so in the very different political context of the city-state of Zurich, within the all but independent Swiss Federation. He first made his mark in 1522 by condemning the traditional practice of fasting in Lent, the Church season that precedes Easter. He then attacked clerical corruption, advocated married priests and rejected the use of images in worship – he wanted churches to be as simple as possible. He preferred the authority of the Bible to that of popes, rejected the sacraments and hoped for a government guided by God's hand. Zwinglism, while influential, has not survived as a distinct movement anywhere outside Switzerland. By contrast, the Frenchman John Calvin (1509–64) is credited with a founding role in modern Presbyterianism. He was based in Geneva, and broke from Rome in 1530, reforming the liturgy, extolling the virtues of the individual's relationship with God, and establishing a new structure for Church governance to replace the authoritarianism of the papacy.

The invention of printing and the Reformation are and remain the two outstanding services of central Europe to the cause of humanity.

Thomas Mann, 1924

As a result, Luther grew in boldness. He rejected five of the seven sacraments that the Church taught, attacked the authority of the Pope and advocated church services in the local language rather than Latin. The breach grew wider. At a gathering in Regentsburg in 1541, there had been hopes of reconciliation, but Luther's demand for married clergy and local independence from the Pope proved too much.

The Church of England By this time, Luther's ideas had spread across Europe and inspired others, including Ulrich Zwingli and John Calvin in Switzerland. In England, Henry VIII (1491–1547) embraced the new Protestant spirit to resolve a dispute with the papacy over divorcing his first wife, who had failed to provide him with a male heir. Subsequent English monarchs swung between extreme Protestantism (Edward VI, 1537–53) and aggressive Catholicism (Mary I, 1516–58) until Henry's second daughter, Elizabeth (1533–1603) built a consensus that eventually resulted in a moderate form of Protestantism, the Church of England.

> **The Church of England, that fine flower of our Island genius for compromise.**
>
> **Robert Bolt, 1960**

Counter-reformation Following the Reformation, the Catholic Church knew that it had to make some changes in order to enable it to survive and regroup. The exact nature of the fightback was decided at the Council of Trent, which met, at intervals, between 1545 and 1563. It re-examined controversial doctrine, insisted on priestly celibacy, upheld the seven sacraments and endorsed the supreme authority of the Pope, but accepted that some of the old abuses had to be stopped. Catholicism was restored in some lands where it had lost influence – France, Poland, the southern Netherlands and parts of Germany – but religious division was ever after part of the face of Europe.

the condensed idea
Roman abuses prompted a revolt

10 The papacy

There are many aspects of Catholicism that set it apart from the rest of Christianity. One of these is its loyalty to the papacy. Catholics believe that the Pope in Rome stands in a direct line that can be traced back to the apostle Peter, and that he has unparalleled spiritual and teaching authority. In certain matters of faith and morals, the Pope speaks infallibly – that is to say, without error.

The hierarchical system of Church government was established by Christianity in CE 160. Up to then, the various Christian communities had enjoyed considerable autonomy, with the result that there was both an absence of clear leadership and frequent disputes over doctrine. To tackle this, the early Church gradually adopted a set-up consisting of a number of clerical layers (archbishops, bishops, priests, deacons), who were governed by the Pope. They in turn wielded authority over the people, who were known as the laity.

Theory and practice In the early years of the Christian Church, the authority of the papacy was something that existed more in theory than in practice. It was not until the middle years of the fifth century, during the papacy of Leo the Great, that the writ of the Pope as Bishop of Rome and successor to St Peter prevailed to any significant extent in Europe. Leo achieved this authority by his personal dedication and example, combined with a successful missionary strategy and alliances with powerful kings and princes.

timeline

CE 64	160
St Peter executed	Hierarchy established

Pope Leo the Great

Leo I (440–461) is one of only two popes in history to be accorded the title 'the Great'. He is best remembered for his insistence on the supreme authority of the papacy in the Church. 'He hammered home the identity of the papacy with Peter,' writes the Cambridge ecclesiastical historian Eamon Duffy. 'Leo's sense of this identity was almost mythical. Leo, though an "unworthy heir", was the inheritor of all Peter's prerogatives.' In applying vigorously and ruthlessly this vision of the papacy, Leo moved Christianity from a system of largely autonomous prelates and bishops, widely scattered about the lands of the old Roman Empire, to a hierarchical model of government with the Pope at the top. A skilled orator and diplomat, he was also a man of great courage. In 452, he confronted Attila the Hun, who was laying waste to northern Italy and preparing to head south towards Rome, and persuaded him to withdraw.

Thereafter there were periods of supreme papal power, and other periods – as in the Dark Ages of the ninth century – when Rome and the papacy fell into disarray. Though Catholicism continues to cling to the notion of an apostolic succession that links every one of St Peter's 260-plus successors back through him to Jesus, the reality is that libertines, frauds and even, legend has it, a woman disguised as a man have held the office. The Church, however, teaches that the failings of

You are Peter and on this rock I will build my church.
Matthew 16

> ❝The Papacy is not other
> than the ghost of the deceased
> Roman Empire.❞

Thomas Hobbes, 1651

individual popes should not detract from the authority of the post. It should also be remembered that many popes have been men of great intellect, humility, spirituality and moral courage, truly worthy of St Peter's mantle.

Papal elections In the Church's first millennium, popes were often elected by popular acclaim – either by the clerics surrounding them, or by the people of Rome. Secular rulers also sometimes played a role, as part of the crucial relationship between Church and state. From 1059 onwards, the system that still exists today began to be established. Popes are now chosen in a series of secret ballots by the Church's cardinals from among their number. Almost 80 per cent of those men who have so far sat on the throne of St Peter have been Italians, and 38 per cent Romans. However, with an ever-larger proportion of cardinal electors now coming from the developing world, it is thought to be only a matter of time before one of their number becomes pope, and thus a symbol of what is now geographically a universal church.

Infallibility The claim to supreme, God-given authority has been made by and of popes through the ages and lies at the very core of Catholicism. What the Pope teaches, it is said, should not be contradicted or ignored by any member of the Church. The tradition that the papacy preserves the truth of the apostles was first enshrined in 519 in the Formula of Hormisdas, named after the pope who, together with the Roman Emperor Justin, endorsed it.

Over the following centuries there was a long-running debate within the Church about papal infallibility, but it was only in the nineteenth century – at precisely the time when the Pope's temporal power was at its lowest ebb, with the loss of the Papal States in 1870 during the push towards the reunification of Italy – that the claim of the Pope to speak without error on some questions in the spiritual domain was endorsed by a meeting of the cardinals in Rome. Since that time, only one papal statement – the declaration in 1950 that Jesus's mother Mary had risen body and soul to heaven, an event known as the Assumption – has been deemed infallible.

Excommunication

In medieval times – when the Inquisition was at the height of its powers, working often through torture and capital punishment to keep Catholics in line with papal teaching – excommunication was used frequently in response to dissent. Post-Reformation, though, the Council of Trent sought to curb such excesses, ordering that excommunication only be invoked with 'sobriety and great circumspection'. The rulebook of the Catholic Church, the Code of Canon Law, includes in its list of sins risking excommunication: apostasy, heresy, schism, desecration of the Eucharist, physical violence against the Pope and procurement of a completed abortion.

Through the workings of his civil service in the Vatican (the curia), the network of local archbishops and bishops around the globe, and priests in parishes, the Pope retains the power to discipline individual Catholics – sometimes by exclusion from the sacraments – and in rare cases to expel them from the Church, in a process known as excommunication. It is stressed, however, that since to be ejected from the Church you must first have joined it through baptism, the door always remains open after excommunication for repentance and readmittance.

the condensed idea
The Pope runs Catholicism

11 Guilt and misogyny

In the four gospels of the New Testament, Jesus concentrates on what might be termed social morality – how individuals and societies should relate to one another in fairness, justice and love. He has very little to say about gender or sexual morality. The Christian Church has throughout its history been led exclusively by men, who continue in some of its branches to refuse to allow women to be ordained as priests. Furthermore, its conservative teaching on contraception, abortion, sex before marriage and homosexuality often overshadows its radical social gospel.

Over the centuries, many of the traditional Western attitudes to sexual morality and the roles within society of men and woman have been shaped by Christianity. While our increasingly secular society has adopted a more permissive attitude, however, the churches have remained faithful to their long-standing teaching, and are often seen today as hostile to sex and prejudiced against women.

Religion, its critics say, is a way of men exerting their control. For many sincere believers, the widening gap between the ideals of their religion concerning sex and gender and the realities of their everyday lives has caused anguish and guilt – as chronicled in the novels of writers such as Graham Greene, Edna O'Brien, Antonia White and David Lodge.

timeline

4th century BCE
Plato sees body and soul as separate

5th century CE
Augustine warns of dangers of sex

Women in Islam and Judaism

There is a contrast in Islam between teaching and practice in relation to women. The Qur'an stresses that men and women are equal, that all originate from a single soul. Historians point out that Muhammad consulted his wives and gave women more rights than had hitherto been traditional. However, in some Muslim countries today women enjoy few rights and freedoms, though whether this is out of choice or because of male prejudice is disputed. The Taliban fundamentalists in Afghanistan, for example, denied women education and insisted that they cover their bodies and faces when out in public, while in Saudi Arabia, women are not allowed to drive cars. Iraq, however, has one of the highest proportions of women in parliament of any country in the world. In Judaism too there is a range of attitudes to women, depending on the particular form of the faith that is prevalent. Some Liberal Jewish congregations, for example, have female rabbis. More Orthodox groups, though, will require women to sit in a separate gallery or area in the synagogue, while in ultra-Orthodox circles women are expected to follow ritual purity laws that include a bar on marital sex during menstruation and prescribe the covering of their hair when in public.

Only in the last hundred years have most Christian denominations begun to allow women to become priests and ministers. In 1853 Antoinette Brown became the first female Congregational minister, in 1886 Helenor Alter Davisson the first Methodist, and in 1942 Florence Li Tim-Oi the first Anglican. The Church of England itself waited until 1992 to ordain women. In the US and New Zealand provinces of

> **My chief difficulties about the Church centre around her attitude to sex. So a case could evidently be made out for the Church being an alternative to sexual life.**
>
> **Antonia White, 1899–1980**

13th century CE
Thomas Aquinas on natural law

19th century CE
First women priests

worldwide Anglicanism there were female bishops from 1989, but some parts of the Communion continue to bar women priests on account of their gender, as does Catholicism. The arguments for doing so are threefold: that Jesus chose only male apostles; that the priest stands in place of Jesus at the altar and must therefore be a man like him; and that the tradition of the Church rules out women priests, even though there is nothing explicit in the gospels.

Catholicism also insists that its priests be celibate (though rare exceptions have been allowed). This was not the practice of the early Church; indeed, right up to the Council of Trent there were married priests. What prompted the ruling was the belief that celibate monks living in monasteries were better examples to the faithful than a local priest with a wife and family. The Catholic hierarchy believed that dependants would distract a priest from his ministry, though other churches have found that being a father and a Father can be successfully combined.

Augustine and Aquinas

St Augustine (354–430) was baptized a Christian but drifted away from the Church during a debauched and worldly youth. At the age of 33, he returned to the fold, encouraged by his mother, St Monica, and spent the rest of his life as an admired bishop and teacher in North Africa. His writings – particularly the *Confessions* and *City of God* – have endured in Catholic circles. Drawing on his own past, Augustine dwelt at length on the sinfulness of human flesh and the dangers for the spirit of human sexuality. St Thomas

Aquinas (1225–74), like Augustine still much quoted by popes and bishops, turned to the writings of the Greek philosophers to construct a rational understanding of God as the creator and source of all being, goodness and truth. His *Summa Theologica* described a natural law, a preordained moral pattern of behaviour, seen in animals but present in humans too. This informed his writings on human sexuality. 'The state of virginity,' he claimed, 'is preferable to that of even continent marriage.'

❛I declare that the Church has no authority whatsoever to confer priestly ordination on women and that this judgement is to be definitively held by all the Church's faithful.❜

Pope John Paul II, 1994

Dangers of sex Christianity was not the first religion to regard sexual pleasure as dangerous. The Greek philosopher Plato (424–348 BCE) taught that the human body was evil because it distracted the mind from the pursuit of truth. He saw sex simply as a function of the body. His pupil Aristotle (384–322 BCE) shared this view, regarding women as inferior to men and too ready to use sex to distract them from cerebral matters. Both Aristotle and Plato were central in shaping the pessimistic note that pervades much of Christian teaching on sexual morality. St Augustine and St Thomas Aquinas in particular used these philosophers' writings as the basis for their own landmark contributions on the subject in the fifth and thirteenth centuries respectively.

Most Christian churches continue to teach that homosexuality is sinful – though Jesus makes no mention of it in the gospels. They also uphold his stated injunction against divorce, one of the few times he does touch on a subject of sexual morality, and most advocate abstaining from sexual relations before marriage. The Catholic Church is opposed to so-called 'artificial contraception' – the Pill, condoms, IUDs – because it believes they interfere with 'the transmission of human life', which is the primary purpose of sex. That unbreakable link between sex and the creation of new life is also what informs Catholicism's hostility to homosexuality.

the condensed idea
Women and sex
are dangerous

12 The Holy Spirit

Mainstream Christianity teaches that there are three persons in the one God – God the Father, God the Son and God the Holy Spirit. Collectively they are known as the Holy Trinity. All three are equal and share the same 'essence', but each has a particular role. In the modern Pentecostal movement, it is the Spirit that is the most prominent element of the Trinity, with the 'gifts of the Spirit' believed to have the power to transform lives. For many Christians, though, the Holy Spirit remains an elusive concept.

There is no specific mention in the scriptures of the Holy Trinity. It was only in the early years of the Church that the doctrine began to emerge, and by the third century CE it had been agreed that Father, Son and Holy Spirit (also known as the Holy Ghost) were not just linked or related but possessed an identical essence. In the the Nicene Creed, the shared statement of faith of many branches of Christianity, laid down in the fourth century, the exact relationship between the elements of the Trinity is spelt out. In the version of the Creed still used in the modern Catholic mass, for instance, worshippers state: 'We believe in the Holy Spirit, the Lord, the giver of life, who proceeds from the Father and the Son. With the Father and the Son he is worshipped and glorified. He has spoken through the prophets.'

Heresy and controversy The formula of the Holy Trinity has proved controversial in Christian history. In the fourth century, Arius, a priest of Alexandria, taught that Jesus was supernatural but not the

timeline
3rd century CE — Doctrine of Trinity emerges
4th century CE — Arian controversy

The first Pentecost

According to John's gospel, on the evening of the day when he rose from the dead, Jesus came amongst the disciples, who had been in hiding since his crucifixion. 'Receive the Holy Spirit,' he said to them. 'For those whose sins you forgive, they are forgiven; for those whose sins you retain, they are retained.' The Acts of the Apostles, which comes later in the New Testament narrative and tells the story of the early years of the Christian Church, describes a similar event happening after Jesus's ascension into heaven. Again the apostles were assembled together in a room, when they heard 'a powerful wind from heaven, the noise of which filled the entire house in which they were sitting; and something appeared to them that seemed like tongues of fire'. Each was filled with the Holy Spirit and could suddenly speak fluently in foreign languages they had never learned. This event is celebrated each year by Christians seven weeks after Easter Sunday as Pentecost, and has given its name to the Pentecostal movement, which believes that the same gifts of the Spirit are available to all believers. Pentecost Sunday is sometimes referred to as the birthday of the Church.

equal of God the Father. The resulting 'Arian heresy' divided the Church. In the ninth century, Eastern Christians opted to omit the 'and the Son' (*filioque* in Latin) from the Creed, insisting that the Spirit proceeded only from the Father. This stance contributed to the schism of 1054 between East and West. In more recent times, some Christian groups, such as the Mormons, have rejected the Trinity altogether, seeing Father, Son and Spirit as three separate persons, united in purpose but not in essence.

1054
Split with East

c.1900
Pentecostalism develops

In both Aramaic – the language that Jesus would have spoken – and Hebrew, the word for 'spirit' is feminine. This has led many Christian thinkers through the ages to see the Holy Spirit as the female aspect of the Godhead.

Tongues of fire Depictions of the Holy Spirit in Christian art have taken several forms. In the gospel accounts of Jesus's baptism in the river Jordan by his cousin John, the Spirit is said to descend on him like

The gift of tongues

Among the gifts of the Holy Spirit referred to in the New Testament is the 'gift of tongues', also called glossolalia. Those who have received this gift can speak in a language that is unrecognizable to their hearers. Christians believe that this phenomenon mirrors the experience of the apostles when the Spirit came upon them. A much smaller number of the faithful, it is said, receive a second gift from the Spirit that enables them to interpret these outpourings. The gift of tongues is regarded by Pentecostal Christians – a movement that grew up in the twentieth century – as the authentic mark of baptism in the Spirit. Pentecostalists describe what is said by those experiencing the gift of tongues as heavenly language, the language of angels, or the language of the Spirit. Academic efforts to decode it have so far yielded few results, though studies have pointed out that those in mid-flow tend to be in a heightened emotional state. The gift of tongues was little known in the earlier centuries of the Church, with St Augustine suggesting that it was a phenomenon limited only to the original apostles. However, certain Christian saints and mystics – including Patrick, the fourth-century patron saint of Ireland – have described communicating with the Spirit in a language that they could understand but which would have been unintelligible to other hearers.

‘Come Holy Ghost, our souls inspire, and lighten with celestial fire. Thou the anointing Spirit art, who dost thy seven-fold gifts impart.’

Book of Common Prayer, 1662

> **❝I sincerely believe that any man preaching a simple Gospel message in the power of the Spirit can expect results if he is speaking to unconverted people.❞**
> **Billy Graham, 1918–**

a dove. This symbol is also seen in representations of the Spirit coming to Mary when an angel tells her she is pregnant with God's son. And in the Acts of the Apostles, the Spirit is shown to Jesus's apostles as a wind or tongues of fire, often depicted by artists as a flame.

Gifts of the Holy Spirit Mainstream Christianity continues to believe that the Holy Spirit has a unique role to play in bringing individuals to conversion, in shaping scripture (hence the reference in the Creed to 'speaking through the prophets') and in helping believers to find the words to speak to others of their faith. According to Catholicism, the Spirit intervenes in the life of the Church primarily to influence its decisions. So when, for example, the cardinals gather to elect a new pope, they are said to cast their votes under the guidance of the Spirit. Protestantism also allocates an institutional function to the Spirit, but prefers to speak of it/her having a direct relationship with individual believers.

In his First Letter to the Corinthians, written around CE 50, St Paul describes the gifts that the Spirit bestowed on individuals. 'One may have the gift of preaching with wisdom given him by the Spirit; another may have the gift of preaching instruction given him by the same Spirit; and another the gift of faith given by the same Spirit; one, the power of miracles; another the gift of tongues and another the ability to interpret them. All of these are the work of one and the same Spirit, who distributes different gifts to different people just as he chooses.'

the condensed idea
God is three in one

13 Saints and sinners

Many religions hold up the example of holy men and women from the past as a means of guiding and inspiring current believers to lead good and moral lives. The Christian Church calls such role models saints, and Catholicism in particular continues to operate a formal system that adds to their number each year.

There are an estimated 10,000 saints already recognized officially who can be called upon in prayer by believers as they search for inspiration, strength and succour in times of trouble. Some saints are said to have a particular concern or patronage: St Joseph, the husband of the Virgin Mary, is the patron saint of carpenters; St Cecilia of music; while St Jude is prayed to by those who feel themselves to be in a desperate situation. From its earliest years the Church has embraced the concept of a 'communion of saints', reborn in heaven, marked out by their haloes (rings of light around their heads in traditional depictions) and acting as intermediaries between humanity and God. Hence individuals are still given a saint's name at baptism, when they formally join the Church, and later, in some branches of the Christian family, choose a saint as their patron at the sacrament of confirmation.

Before 1234, the process of saint-making was carried out across Christianity by popular acclaim. It was believed that the life story of a highly esteemed individual could offer a glimpse of what God was like.

timeline

c.35 CE	4th century
Death of Stephen, first saint	Haloes appear in Christian art

Haloes

The use of haloes in religious art pre-dates Christianity. A ring of light above the head to signify a deity can be seen in ancient Egyptian and Asian depictions, as well as in portrayals of Greek and Roman gods. Christianity first took up the practice around the fourth century; originally it was only for pictures of Jesus, but the practice quickly spread. There is a hierarchy of haloes in Christian art. Triangular ones are reserved for the three persons of the Trinity – Father, Son and Holy Spirit. Round haloes – in white, gold or yellow – are for saints. The Virgin Mary has a circle of stars, though some artists would give her a mandorla – or all-body halo. A square halo would be used when depicting a living but saintly figure – as, for example, in paintings of various popes. Judas is traditionally given a black halo. The practice of depicting saints with haloes began to die out in the Renaissance period.

This was particularly true of those who were martyred for their faith in the early years of Christianity. Stephen, a Jewish convert and deacon, is reported by the Acts of the Apostles to have been stoned to death because of his missionary work. He is regarded by Christianity as the first saint, and his powers as a preacher and miracle-worker might be seen as setting the template for all subsequent saints.

This democratic system could be erratic. Often stories of different individuals would end up conflated. There are, for example, a clutch of early female saints (Pelagia, Apollinaris, Euphrosyne, Eugenia, Marina) who dressed as men to achieve ascetic lives and whose stories bear a remarkable similarity. Equally, some early saints – Christopher, beloved of drivers, or Valentine, patron of lovers – are now thought not to have existed at all. Their biographies were based on earlier pagan gods, who had been subsumed into the early Christian Church.

As the leaders of the Church became more active in regulating the lives of the faithful, the process of saint-making was taken under official control. In 1234, Pope Gregory IX claimed for the Bishop of Rome absolute power over recognizing saints. From this point onwards, the

Modern saints

Mother Teresa of Calcutta (1910–97) was an Albanian-born Catholic nun who earned worldwide praise for her work with the poor, the dispossessed and the dying in India. She founded a flourishing religious order, the Missionaries of Charity, who wear her distinctive blue-edged white robes. She was awarded the Nobel Peace Prize in 1979. Six years after her death, she was beatified by Pope John Paul II. Monsignor Josemaria Escriva (1902–75) was the Spanish founder of the Opus Dei movement within Catholicism. Its conservative approach and tendency to secrecy makes it highly controversial (notably in Dan Brown's novel *The Da Vinci Code*), but Escriva was canonized in 2002, just 27 years after his death. By contrast, Archbishop Oscar Romero (1917–80), though considered a saint by many in his native Central America, still awaits official recognition. His outspoken attacks on the violation of basic human rights by the Salvadorean military government were silenced when he was gunned down by soldiers at the altar as he said mass in March 1980. His martyrdom was not sufficient to prompt the Catholic Church to speed up the process of canonization because, it is thought, Rome feared a political interpretation being placed on its actions.

❝The saints have always been the source and origin of renewal in the most difficult moments in the Church's history.❞

Catechism of the Catholic Church, 1994

range of candidates elevated to sainthood became narrower, and greater proof was demanded both of their virtues in life, and of some miraculous intervention after death.

Modern saint-making It is Catholicism that today devotes most energy to saint-making. The Orthodox Church, by contrast, prefers to see saints not as moral models but simply as individuals who are now in heaven. It respects the fact that people may remember them as exceptional figures, but it does not pass judgement on them. Anglicans and other of the Protestant denominations recognize the major figures in Christian history as saints, but have no formal process for adding to their number. Methodism warns against the veneration of saints altogether.

> ❛To most, even good people, God is a belief. To the saints, he is an embrace.❜
>
> **Francis Thompson, 1859–1907**

Integral to the Catholic process of saint-making is the necessity for miracles. To become a saint, an individual must be shown, to the satisfaction of the Church authorities, to have answered the prayers of the faithful from beyond the grave. The most straightforward proof is if someone who has been praying to the would-be saint is miraculously cured of an illness. In the present system, proof of one miracle is required for the candidate to be beatified – declared blessed – and of two for them to be canonized – named a saint.

Between 1234 and 1978, there were fewer than 300 successful candidates for sainthood. The Church's habit was to ponder long and hard on its decisions – often taking more than a century to reach a verdict – and to promote only those of exceptional virtue. Pope John Paul II (1978–2005) took a different approach. In total, he created 476 saints and approved 1,315 beatifications.

the condensed idea
You can't beat a good role model

14 Orthodoxy

The phrase 'was, is, will be', taken from prayers used in the Orthodox liturgy, summarises the belief of this major Christian tradition that it alone has preserved the ancient structures of the early Church and the faith of the apostles. 'Orthodox' translates as 'right teaching'. In their theology, their decision-making and above all their liturgies, the three main branches that together comprise Eastern Orthodoxy – the Greek, the Russian and the various Balkan strands – regard themselves as unchanging over two millennia.

With around 250 million adherents around the world, Orthodoxy is the largest single group within Christianity after Catholicism. The origins of the split between Western and Eastern Christianity lie in the divisions of the old Roman Empire. While the Western section, based on Rome itself, fell in the fifth century, the Eastern part, with its capital Constantinople, persisted in various forms right up to 1453, when it was overrun by the Ottomans. The Christian Church reflected this political divide with a patriarch based in Constantinople who regarded himself as the equal of the Bishop of Rome and resisted the papacy's claim to universal authority over Christians. The Eastern Church even tried to trump the claim of Rome to have a direct line back to Jesus through St Peter by declaring that it had been founded by Andrew, the first-recruited among Christ's apostles.

Schism of 1054 It was against this backdrop that the various theological disputes that contributed to the East–West Schism of 1054

timeline

381
Council of Constantinople sets up city's patriarchate

c.540
Rebuilding of Hagia Sophia (Holy Wisdom), mother church of Orthodoxy, now a mosque

Saints Cyril and Methodius

Cyril (*c.*827–869) and Methodius (*c.*815–885), known as the Apostles to the Slavs, were Greek-speaking brothers who brought Christianity to the peoples of Eastern Europe, the Balkans and beyond. To make it easier to translate the Bible for their new converts, they devised their own Slavonic language, which remains in use in Orthodox churches to this day. They are venerated by Orthodoxy as the equals of the original apostles. In 868, they are believed to have travelled to Rome, where they were warmly welcomed by the Pope. Catholicism includes them in its calendar of saints and Pope John Paul II declared them patrons of Europe.

were played out. Among the issues that divided the two sides were attitudes to the Trinity (see page 49), the Eastern Church's attachment to the use of icons, and disputes over the Eucharist and liturgical arrangements. There had been numerous breaches before 1054 but these had always been repaired, and many hoped that the rift could once again be healed. However, the sacking of Constantinople in 1204 by Crusaders sent by the Pope to fight in the Holy Land, along with attempts to set up a Latin (Roman) patriarchate in the region, scuppered any hopes of a reconciliation. Further efforts were made in 1274 and 1439; the latter, at the Council of Florence, enjoyed some success before external events intervened in 1453, when Constantinople fell to its Ottoman attackers.

Separation from Rome led to a widening of the differences between the Western and Eastern parts of Christianity, especially after 1453, when the Balkan and Greek strands of the Orthodox Church were to embark on 400 years under Islamic overlordship. The

> **Its members [are] images of God in all respects, clear and spotless mirrors, reflecting the glow of primordial light and indeed of God himself.**
>
> **Dionysius the Areopagite, late 5th century**

1054
East and West split

1453
Constantinople falls to Ottomans

> **Jesus was made man that we might be made God.**
>
> **St Athanasius of Alexandria,** *c.***293–373**

Reformation and all the upheavals that followed effectively passed them by. With the fall of Constantinople, the power base of the Eastern Church passed to Moscow, which referred to itself as 'the third Rome'.

In the twentieth century, following the Russian Revolution of 1917 and the Soviet takeover of much of Eastern Europe in the wake of the Second World War, the Orthodox Church was battered into submission by hostile communist authorities (according to some estimates, around six million Russian Orthodox Christians lost their lives because of their faith). It managed to remain in operation only by focusing narrowly on liturgy and worship and absenting itself from any involvement in the affairs of wider society.

Devolved authority The modern Orthodox Church has no single leader with a status to rival the Pope. The Ecumenical Patriarch of Constantinople presides as the first among equals at gatherings of Orthodox bishops from the three main branches. Orthodoxy's structure of authority is also much more devolved, in line with the practice of the early Christian communities. Local bishops have authority within their area, and gather with other bishops from the region to take decisions on matters of broader concern.

The Orthodox priesthood is open to married men, but bishops must be celibate and are drawn largely from the powerful monastic tradition within Orthodoxy. Great emphasis is placed on the 'Holy Tradition' of the Church in terms of teaching. The prime purpose of each individual in Orthodoxy is *theosis* – the mystical union of human beings with God at both a collective and an individual level.

Ancient liturgies The most tangible distinction between Orthodoxy and Western Christianity can be seen in the former's majestic style of worship. Neither the furnishings nor the rituals in Orthodox churches have changed much in a thousand years. Clouds of incense accompany divine liturgy. Priests are clad in ornate robes, and sport beards and long hair in imitation of the apostles. Icons – or

Icons

Orthodoxy has a prescribed artistic convention regarding icons, although it varies between the different traditions within the Church. In general, it is believed that icons should not – as they do in Western religious art – show the human side of Jesus, his mother or the saints, but instead should depict their divine life. Within the Russian, Greek and various Balkan strands of the Church, there are well-established symbolic codes for icons. In the Russian tradition, for instance, the Virgin Mary's clothing is usually shown as a darkish red to symbolize humanity, earth, blood and sacrifice. She is never shown wearing a crown, even though the Orthodox regard her as Queen of Heaven, because a crown would be too human. Often three stars are added to her robes to denote before, during and after the virgin birth. In the early centuries of Christianity, all icon painters would have been monks, and the tradition lives on that icon-painting is a form of devotion, with the artistic endeavour accompanied by prayer and contemplation. The Orthodox believe that St Luke, one of the four gospel writers, was the first to paint Jesus's mother. Though icons largely fell out of use in Western Christianity after the split with the East, some religious artists such as Duccio in the Italian Renaissance and El Greco in sixteenth- and seventeenth-century Spain did produce them, albeit with Western ideas diluting the strict Orthodox rules.

religious paintings – are placed around the church and surrounded by candles. The congregation bows before the icons and kisses them. An elaborate screen, or iconostatis, separates the altar and hence the clergy from the body of the church and the laity. Much of the liturgy is chanted. There is a distinct choreography of movement and gesture to the whole service, which can last for several hours. The few pews available are restricted to the elderly and infirm. Orthodoxy has steadfastly refused to update its liturgical arrangements and forms of words, which it believes continue to mirror those of the early centuries of Christianity and to reflect the timelessness of heaven.

the condensed idea
Christian history isn't only about Rome

15 Luther and his successors

The word Protestant was first used at the Diet of Speyer in 1529 to describe those who questioned the authority of Rome. It was 12 years after Martin Luther had sparked the Reformation with his rebellion against the papacy (see Chapter 9). Over the subsequent centuries, the term has been applied to a variety of denominations, including Lutherans, Presbyterians, Baptists and Anglicans. What unites these groups is an emphasis on individual study of the Bible, simplicity of worship and a belief in the importance of preaching. All these features can be traced back to Luther's original dispute with Rome.

A variety of factors enabled Luther to break the stranglehold on Western Christianity of the Roman Church. Among them was the rise of nationalism in Europe. Rulers and, to a lesser extent, their people were no longer willing to be dictated to by the Pope and his ally the Holy Roman Emperor. This political, nationalist dimension fuelled the initial spread of Luther's ideas – and eventually his new church – throughout Germany and beyond, notably into Scandinavia, where it was taken up by both the Danish and Swedish royal families, who between them ruled the entire region.

The growth of national Lutheran churches, however, posed a challenge to maintaining a single set of beliefs. Initially the new churches united in signing up to the Augsburg Confession in 1530, and during his

timeline

1517	1530
Luther's Ninety-Five Theses	Augsburg Confession

lifetime Luther remained a focus for them all, superseding the influence of individual rulers. At his right hand was Philipp Melanchthon, who, though he lacked Luther's gifts as a leader and a preacher, brought intellectual backbone and theological order to the emerging church. 'I had to fight with rabble and devils, for which reason my books are very warlike,' Luther wrote in the preface to one of Melanchthon's books. 'I am the rough pioneer who must break the road; but Master Philipp comes along softly and gently, sows and waters heartily, since God has richly endowed him with gifts.'

In the decades that followed Luther's death in 1546, disagreements and divisions broke out. This period of turbulence, exacerbated by the efforts of the Catholic Counter-Reformation, resulted in a compromise in 1580, when most Lutherans signed up to the Book of Concord, a clear statement of the beliefs that united them.

Lutheran principles The Book of Concord identified the key and enduring elements of Luther's reform programme. Notable among these was the emphasis on *sola scriptura*, the supremacy of the Bible over any traditional or 'man-made' teaching of the Church. It was agreed that the Bible had been written under the influence of the Holy Spirit and that it, rather than the Pope, represented the ultimate authority in Christianity. One of Luther's greatest achievements was to translate the Bible from Latin into German so that it was more accessible. Another key principle was *sola fide*, sometimes also called 'justification by faith alone', which holds that human salvation comes via faith in God, and is not earned or influenced by good works, as is believed by Catholics.

> **Whatever your heart clings to and confides in, that is really your God.**
>
> **Martin Luther, 1529**

Of the Protestant churches that grew out of the Reformation, Lutheranism is the oldest and remains one of the closest to Catholicism. It accepts the sacraments – though most Lutherans favour only two, as opposed to the seven taught by Rome – but places them beneath preaching in the hierarchy of truths. It has bishops and monks, and while it prefers a plainer style of worship, this still includes music (Johann Sebastian Bach composed for the Lutheran Church).

The Book of Concord

This historic document, made up of ten separate sections, is the unifying force in world Lutheranism. It was agreed in Dresden in 1580 to mark the fiftieth anniversary of the original Augsburg Confession, where Luther and his followers had set out their beliefs in a series of theses. It was compiled by Jakob Andreae and Martin Chemnitz, and was an attempt to maintain coherence between the various parts of what was then a fast-growing church. It begins by stating that Lutheranism stands in a direct line back to the principles and practices of the early Christian Church, and that it – rather than Rome – is the true inheritor of the spirit of that Church. As well as the Augsburg Confession itself, it includes the Small and Large Catechisms of Martin Luther, plus various of his other writings and sermons. All new Lutheran ministers must pledge unconditionally to uphold the Book of Concord.

Pietist practice In the eighteenth century, the conservatism of mainstream Lutheranism provoked opposition from within. The Pietist movement urged greater radicalism and an abandonment of the trappings of 'Catholic' religion in favour of a deeper personal commitment to practising in everyday life what the Bible taught. The Pietists are said to have inspired John Wesley to found the Methodist movement (see Chapter 17).

> **Faith is nothing else than trust in the divine mercy promised in Christ.**
>
> Philipp Melanchthon, 1497–1560

Pietism

The continuing attachment of the Lutheran Church to the sacraments and to a traditional style of worship came under sustained attack in the late seventeenth and eighteenth centuries from the Pietists. As its name suggests, this movement wanted to promote a more austere and individual type of piety, concentrating on repeated reading of the Bible and on living a simple, Godly life that rejected worldly pleasures. Its leading light was the Lutheran pastor Philip Jacob Spener (1637–1705), whose book *Pia Desideria* inspired many others, among them August Francke (1663–1727). A professor at the University of Halle, the intellectual home of Pietism, Francke is best remembered today as a founder of schools for the poor. Another Pietist, the theologian Heinrich Muller (1631–75), castigated the presence in Lutheran churches of the confessional, the altar, the baptismal font and the pulpit as 'four dumb idols', favouring instead gatherings for Bible study and prayer at 'colleges of piety'.

There are an estimated 64 million Lutherans in the world. The biggest concentration continues to be in Germany and Scandinavia, and Lutheranism is the state religion in Denmark, Iceland and Norway. There are also sizeable Lutheran populations in the United States and in former German colonies such as Namibia. In line with many other churches, Lutheranism is acquiring large numbers of new recruits in both Africa and Asia, as the Christian map of the world continues to reshape itself.

the condensed idea
Read the Bible more

16 Anglicanism

In England, the Reformation took its own particular form. It was dictated in part by political circumstances – the Pope's refusal to allow Henry VIII to divorce his wife and the King's resulting determination to set up a national church that would allow him to have his own way – but there was also a religious motive, with the influence of Luther and Calvin making itself felt in England as elsewhere in Europe. The new Church of England eventually positioned itself between Protestantism and Catholicism. It maintains formal links with the state and has expanded, hand-in-hand with the British Empire, across the globe. Today there is an 80-million-strong Anglican Communion, the third largest Christian grouping in the world.

The theological basis of the Church of England was originally defined in the Thirty-Nine Articles of 1563. These represent the culmination of a series of attempts to lay down the distinctive beliefs of the national church. The process began under Henry VIII in 1536 with 10 articles putting a modest distance between the new church and Rome. The gap widened in 1552 with a fresh set of 42 articles, drawn up by one of the most Protestant-leaning of English Reformation figures, Thomas Cranmer, Archbishop of Canterbury. The final tally of 39 was the result of a compromise agreed during the reign of Elizabeth I.

Balancing act The tone and composition of the Thirty-Nine Articles demonstrate clearly the balancing act that is Anglicanism.

timeline

1529
Henry VIII declares himself head of English church

1563
Thirty-Nine Articles

The first eight articles are broadly Catholic and look back to the apostles and the practices of the early Church. The next 10 turn to the newer insights of the Reformation but stop short of a full endorsement of matters such as Luther's position on justification by faith alone: Anglicanism leaves room also for good works. The rest concern themselves with doctrine and the position of the Church in relation to the state.

The Book of Common Prayer, the other pillar of Anglicanism, also evolved during this turbulent period. The hand behind much of it was again that of Thomas Cranmer, who also pursued the dissolution of the monasteries, the promotion of services in English rather than Latin, and an end to the veneration of saints and the overabundance of religious imagery in churches. While a key adviser to first Henry VIII and then, after his death in 1547, to his son Edward VI, Cranmer combined words of devotion from the Roman tradition with an interpretation of the sacraments that owed more to Luther and Calvin. After many disputes and revisions, a final text appeared in 1662 and has remained in use ever since, though in 1980 an Alternative Service Book was introduced.

Fault line The fault line in the Church between Catholic and Protestant – or Reformed, as most Anglicans prefer – persists to this day. 'Low' or 'Evangelical' Anglicanism owes much to Luther, Zwingli and Calvin with its simple ceremonies and Bible-centred teachings.

> **When an Anglican is asked, "Where was your church before the Reformation?" his best answer is to put the counter-question, "Where was your face before you washed it?"**
>
> Michael Ramsey, Archbishop of Canterbury, 1961–74

1662	1867	2003
Book of Common Prayer	First Lambeth Conference	First openly gay bishop

The Oxford Movement

In the 1830s, the Oxford Movement (also known as the Tractarians, due to their habit of setting out their views in tracts or booklets) attempted to steer Anglicanism closer to the traditions of the early Church and – its critics said – of Roman Catholicism. Its key figures – John Henry Newman, Edward Pusey and John Keble, all academics at Oxford University – felt that Anglicanism had become too plain and encouraged a return to medieval forms of worship and monasticism. They argued that the Thirty-Nine Articles could be reconciled with the teachings of the Catholic Council of Trent. Newman's conversion to Roman Catholicism in 1845 weakened the movement substantially.

Meanwhile 'High' or 'Anglo-Catholic' Anglicans take their lead from Catholicism when it comes to forms of worship and theology, though most reject the supreme authority of the Pope. In recent times many High Anglicans have joined Roman Catholicism and Orthodoxy in exasperation at their church's ordination of women, and the overstepping of authority they believe this represents. In 2009, the Pope agreed to allow 'Catholic' Anglicans to convert to Rome as parishes or even whole dioceses.

The centre ground in Anglicanism, usually known as the Liberals and traditionally the repository of power in the Communion, has shrunk as it has struggled to hold the worldwide Church together over divisive issues such as female ordination (enthusiastically embraced in some provinces; banned in others) and homosexuality. The policy of no single province moving ahead with reform until all others have been convinced, for the sake of unity, has been abandoned. The election in 2003 of an openly gay bishop, Gene Robinson, in the Episcopalian (Anglican) Church in the United States has caused some African provinces to threaten to break away from the Communion.

> **It has been the wisdom of the Church of England, ever since the first compiling of her Publick Liturgy, to keep the mean between the two extremes, of too much stiffness in refusing, and of too much easiness in admitting any variation from it.**
>
> **Book of Common Prayer, 1662**

Evelyn Underhill and Anglican spirituality

Anglicanism has struggled to develop its own distinctive spirituality, particularly in provinces such as England, where its role as the state religion has required it to appeal to a broad constituency. However, the Wolverhampton-born poet and novelist Evelyn Underhill (1875–1941) attracted a large following in the first decades of the twentieth century with her writings, lectures and retreats. Her most successful book, *Mysticism* (1911), had as its subtitle 'A Study of Man's Nature and the Development of Man's Spiritual Consciousness'. She placed great emphasis on the role of the Holy Spirit, on contemplative (rather than public) prayer, and on the emerging discipline of psychology.

The Archbishop of Canterbury is the leader of the Anglican Communion, but his powers are strictly limited. He presides as first amongst equals over the once-every-ten-years gathering of all Anglican bishops, the Lambeth Conference, which first met in 1867, but can only get his own way by persuasion and consent. Many Anglican provinces – such as the Church of England itself – operate on a similarly democratic model, with key decisions voted for by representatives of the bishops, clergy and laity at regular meetings called synods.

The Church of England remains an established church, though calls for disestablishment have been loud and persistent. Its head is the British monarch, and its bishops are appointed by the state, with some of them sitting in the House of Lords, the upper chamber of Parliament. Anglican doctrine reacts more swiftly to the secular mood than does Roman Catholicism. For example, the Communion does not oppose artificial contraception, and, though it regrets abortion, it does not oppose it being legally available. The Church of England regards the whole English population as being part of its congregation, not just those who are Anglican. It exists therefore as much for those without it as within.

the condensed idea
Struggling towards a middle way

17 Methodism

The founder of Methodism, John Wesley, never intended to start a new church. He remained an Anglican clergyman all his life, but his efforts in the eighteenth century to reform and reinvigorate what he saw as a too comfortable and consequently out-of-touch Church of England resulted in the birth of what is now a 70-million-strong worldwide movement.

In the same way that Pietism grew out of unease with the conservatism of mainstream Lutheranism, so Methodism was a revolt against what Wesley regarded as a lack of passion, vision and engagement, particularly with the needy, on the part of the Church of England. As the established religion, Anglicanism had, he felt, shared too readily in the growing prosperity of an England booming amid the Industrial Revolution. Too many parish churches were offering a warmer welcome to the new factory-owners than to their workers.

'Holy Club' While studying for the priesthood at Oxford, Wesley, the son and grandson of Anglican clergymen, joined a group of like-minded young Evangelical Anglicans known as the 'Holy Club'. Their detractors referred to them as 'Methodists', on account of their methodical approach to life and faith. The group became involved in fasting, Bible study and works of charity amongst prisoners and the poor.

In May 1738, Wesley attended a Pietist service at which he heard some of Martin Luther's words read aloud. He felt his heart 'strangely warmed', and became convinced in that moment of his own mission to

timeline

1738	1791	1795
Wesley hears the call	Wesley dies an Anglican	Methodist Church set up

instil a similar spirit of reform into the Church of England. He wanted Anglicanism, he said, to be 'a religion of the heart'.

In 1739, Wesley set off on a missionary journey round England, preaching the need for a more socially active church. Many of his meetings were held in the open air – 'field preaching' – because the local parish church shunned both him and the working-class crowds he drew. Alongside his oratory there were the rousing hymns of his brother, Charles, who wrote 9,000 of them in total, including 'Love Divine, All Loves Excelling' and 'Hark! the Herald Angels Sing'.

'Four alls' Despite the fact that he attracted criticism from Anglican colleagues, ridicule in the press and even threats to his life, Wesley inspired many other itinerant preachers, some of them women, to follow in his footsteps. Their message was distilled into what

> **O, for a thousand tongues to sing.**
> **Charles Wesley, 1740**

Methodism in America

In the 1760s, Wesley began sending preachers to what were then Britain's American colonies. With the outbreak of the American War of Independence (1775–83), the link between Methodist preachers in the United States and the established Church of England (of which Wesley was still a member) had to be severed. Wesley's solution was to ordain Thomas Coke as the leader of a separate US Methodist Episcopal Church in 1784. From its base in Baltimore, it spread rapidly throughout the country. In the process there was a series of schisms, which were not healed until 1968, when the Methodist Church and the United Brethren Church joined forces as the United Methodist Church, the second largest Protestant denomination in America with around eight million members. It combines Wesley's social gospel with an evangelical style of preaching. Its logo is the flame – the symbol of the Holy Spirit – and it is anti-alcohol, gambling, capital punishment and war.

1810 Primitives split off

1931 Methodist Union

1972 Merger talks with Church of England blocked

Methodism calls the 'four alls' – all need to be saved, all can be saved, all can know they are saved and all can be saved completely.

The elements of high oratory, revivalist fervour and rousing music were eventually combined by Wesley into a Methodist society, still Anglican, but with its own chapels and networks. In the 1760s, some of the society's preachers set off for America. Wesley made repeated efforts to stay within the Anglican fold, and in 1758 he wrote a pamphlet entitled *Reasons Against a Separation from the Church of England*, but he also began ordaining his own ministers. A formal break was inevitable, and came four years after his death in 1791.

Nonconformist When Wesley died, he left behind 57,000 members of his Methodist society. Fifty years later, this number had grown to half a million in Britain and a million in the United States. The new church was often called Nonconformist, because it did not conform to the norms of the Church of England, instead combining elements of Lutheran theology with a High Anglican attachment to the sacraments and a radical social concern. Its principal style of worship was laid out in the Book of Offices, which was based on the 1662 Anglican Book of Common Prayer. Indeed, in the 1960s, Methodism negotiated a reunion with the Church of England, but the move was blocked in 1972 by the Anglicans.

Popular in industrial and mining towns, and among small farmers and agricultural workers, Methodism came in Victorian times to embody what is sometimes called the 'Protestant work ethic' of hard labour and strict morality. It taught the virtues of honesty, thrift and temperance. Gambling was frowned upon, and members of the chapel congregation were constantly encouraged to better themselves materially as well as spiritually.

> **❝Gain all you can. Save all you can, give all you can.❞**
>
> **John Wesley, 1760**

Primitive Methodists

With Wesley's death, and the establishment of Methodism as a separate denomination, the movement lost some of its radicalism. In spite of being described as Nonconformist, it had, some felt, become too conventional. It was the aim of Hugh Bourne and William Clowes, both uneducated artisans, to revive the original zeal through a movement known as Primitive Methodism. They split with the mainstream in 1810 and were condemned as 'ranters' because they held all-day open-air prayer meetings, sang hymns to the tunes of popular songs, carried out healings and miracle cures, and insisted on plain speaking, plain dressing, plain worshipping and plain living. Primitive Methodism prided itself on being a democratic church of the poor for the poor, and it set up small chapels in many industrial towns and countryside villages in a bid to rival the mainstream Methodists. As the century progressed, there were increasing efforts to heal the breach, and in 1931 the two movements were eventually reconciled in the Methodist Union. A separate Primitive Methodist Church continues to exist in the United States.

With the expansion of the British Empire, Methodism was exported around the world with typical vigour and determination. A democratic, devolved international church, it continues to be based around districts and circuits. In most countries it elects its leaders, who hold office for set periods and eschew any personality cult, though in others there are Methodist bishops. It lacks a clear, shared theology and practice, an absence that has made it more vulnerable than other denominations to splits and divisions. In the United States alone, there are currently up to 40 separate churches all using the word Methodist in their title.

the condensed idea
Christianity demands a radical social edge

18 Baptists

In every Christian denomination, baptism marks the moment when an individual joins the church. In a ceremony based on Jesus's baptism by his cousin John, new members are welcomed into the fold. Baptists, though, reject the traditional Christian practice of doing this in infancy. They hold that baptism can only be administered – often by total immersion in water – when an individual is mature enough to make an informed adult commitment to following Christ's example in their life.

There are around 110 million Baptists worldwide, spread among many autonomous churches. What unites them is their particular approach to baptism. On all other matters of doctrine there are distinct differences – and in many cases gulfs – between them. In 2004, for example, the 16-million-strong Southern Baptist Convention in the USA left the church's umbrella body, the Baptist World Alliance, accusing it of being 'too liberal'.

> **One leak will sink a ship, and one sin will destroy a sinner.**
>
> John Bunyan, 1678

The origins of the Baptists can be traced back to the Reformation, when dissenters took the message of Zwingli, Luther and Calvin to heart, but carried it one stage further, arguing that since nowhere in the gospels does Jesus baptize infants, neither would they. The original Reformation leaders opposed this decision, but the 'Baptists' stood their ground, in the process developing a profound dislike of hierarchy and efforts to impose doctrine and conformity on them.

timeline

Anabaptists The historical roots of the Baptists as a movement lie in the Anabaptists, a close relative of the Puritans, who separated from the Church of England in the early seventeenth century, under the influence of John Smyth and Thomas Helwys. This radical group, whose first church is believed to have been founded in 1524 in Augsburg in Germany, came to reject not just infant baptism but all other demands made by secular authority, such as joining armies, attending law courts, taking oaths, and even accepting the right of any prince or king to rule over them. They were as a result regarded as rebels and traitors and suffered prolonged periods of persecution.

The Anabaptist influence was felt in England in the Separatist religious movement – which, as its name implies, rejected any link between religion and the state and therefore repudiated the claims of the Church of England. Among those caught up with Separatism were Smyth and Helwys, In 1609 they were both forced into exile in the Dutch Republic, then a haven for Nonconformists, where they formed an English-speaking congregation that met in the back of a bakery. Smyth led the way by baptizing himself, and developed a body of opinions that have caused him to be described as the founder of the Baptist movement. He rejected all

John Bunyan

John Bunyan was originally a travelling salesman, trudging round English towns and villages selling household wares. He became a Baptist in 1653, when he was immersed in the River Great Ouse, and thereafter developed a national reputation as an itinerant preacher of special persuasion. With the restoration of the monarchy in 1660, in the aftermath of the Civil War and Cromwell's Commonwealth, tolerance of most forms of Protestantism was curtailed. Bunyan refused to conform and insisted on carrying on with his preaching. As a result, from 1660 onwards, he suffered repeated periods of imprisonment. While inside in 1676, he wrote the first draft of *The Pilgrim's Progress*, which reflected in common speech the doubts, temptations and tribulations of everyday life as it mapped the spiritual journey between the 'City of Destruction' and the 'Celestial City'. It remained, until the mid nineteenth century, the most-read book in English after the Bible.

1634
First Baptist congregation in US

1676
Bunyan begins *The Pilgrim's Progress*

1792
Baptist Missionary Society founded

forms of liturgy as coming between believers and God, and advocated a simple twofold leadership structure of pastors and deacons (as opposed to the threefold model favoured in other Protestant denominations).

Right to autonomy In 1612, the Baptists returned to England and founded their first congregation at Spitalfields in east London. Helwys published a book dedicated to King James I arguing that the monarch had no right to rule over the consciences of individuals, 'for men's religion is between God and themselves'. As a result, he was imprisoned and died in jail, the first of a line of Baptist martyrs.

In 1620, Baptists sailed on the *Mayflower* to Massachusetts and founded congregations in the new colony. The organizing principle was democracy. No minister could impose his views on others. Matters had to be decided democratically by each congregation. This belief in individual and local autonomy means that there has never been one single Baptist church, but rather a series of interlinked movements, all of which use the name Baptist.

'**Expect great things from God; attempt great things for God.**'

William Carey, 1793

When the Baptist movement spread to the southern states of America, it was forced to confront the issue of slavery. The majority of Baptists insisted that all men, black or white, were equal before God, but a minority, the Southern Baptist Convention, defended slavery, claiming that it was justified by the Bible, and split off. In Britain by this time, Baptists had become accepted by the establishment, and were in the forefront of the battle to abolish the slave trade, seeing in the treatment of blacks a parallel with their own earlier persecution as religious dissenters.

In 1792, the Baptist Missionary Society was founded in London to bring the Baptist message to India and the East. Among its best-known members was William Carey (1761–1834), a cobbler by trade, who spent the last 40 years of his adult life in India, where he translated the Bible into 25 different local languages and dialects.

Believers' baptism

What continues to unite all Baptists to this day is their emphasis on what they call 'believers' baptism', to distinguish it from the practice of infant baptism. (In some Baptist churches, children are not allowed to attend at all, and in most they cannot be full members until they reach their teenage years.) Baptism is not seen as the moment when an individual is 'born again', as in other Evangelical groups, but rather as the public expression of an inner commitment to God. So immersion in water has a threefold symbolism – washing away the old life, being resurrected in a new life with God, and living out that faith every day.

> ## Spelling out what it is to be a Baptist
>
> Baptists sometimes use the name of the denomination as an acronym to spell out their core beliefs: **B**iblical authority; **A**utonomy of the local church; **P**riesthood of all believers; **T**wo ordinances (sacraments, by any other name, of baptism and eucharist); **I**ndividual soul liberty; **S**eparation of Church and state; and **T**wo offices of the church (pastor and deacon).

Another shared perspective for Baptists is what are often called the four freedoms – of the individual's soul, of church (the ability to worship wherever and in whatever form you choose), of the Bible (to interpret it as you see fit) and of religion (to pick your own way to God rather than have it imposed by your local overlord). However, all these points of convergence are lived out in different ways in the various Baptist congregations. So there are, for example, 50 separate Baptist churches in the United States alone, while in some countries Baptists favour what is called 'open membership' – allowing individuals who are part of another denomination to worship with them, sometimes without even requiring that they go through believers' baptism. In this way they are truly putting into practice those freedoms they believe in so strongly.

the condensed idea
Only adults can commit to Christ

19 Presbyterians

A number of churches that grew out of the Protestant Reformation took as their inspiration John Calvin rather than Martin Luther. These are collectively known as Presbyterian or Reformed. Calvin was more radical than Luther in his break with past practice in church organization and liturgy, rejecting decoration in churches, ceremony and almost all music in services, as well as the office of bishop. This resulted in Presbyterianism developing as an austere, simple but dignified style of worship with a deep spirituality. The movement is followed by around 24 million people globally, and is found in significant numbers in Scotland, Holland, Switzerland and the United States.

Among Calvin's innovations was his creation of the role of elder, a non-cleric who was involved in both the democratic decision-making process of the church and the provision of pastoral care. He – and originally elders were all men – was a priest/minister without being ordained. Indeed, the origin of the word Presbyterian lies in the Greek for 'elder' – *presbyteros*. In the early Church, Calvin argued, quoting the Acts of the Apostles, there were lay elders who were the equal of clerical bishops: 'In each of these churches, they appointed elders, and with prayer and fasting, they commanded them to the Lord in whom they had come to believe.'

Spread of Presbyterianism Presbyterianism spread rapidly from Calvin's Geneva base. Among those profoundly influenced by his teaching was John Knox, who travelled to Switzerland and worked

timeline

1559	1560
Calvin's Institute of Christian Religion completed	Kirk established

under him. When he later returned to his native Scotland (at that time a separate kingdom from England and Wales), Knox was prominent in the rebellion that broke out in 1558 over the marriage of the young monarch, Mary, Queen of Scots, to the Catholic heir to the French throne. He eventually persuaded the Scottish Parliament of 1560 to adopt Calvinism as the national Church of Scotland, popularly known as the Kirk. Even after the 1707 Act of Union, which disbanded the Scottish Parliament in favour of a single legislature in London, the Presbyterian Church of Scotland remained the established church north of the border, as Anglicanism wass to the south.

John Knox

Had it not been for John Knox (c.1510–72), the Church of Scotland might well have ended up Anglican, as in England, rather than Presbyterian. Given that it was the existence of a Presbyterian national church in Scotland that inspired many Reformed believers – not least the Puritans who travelled to the United States – Knox has a strong claim to be counted alongside Calvin as one of the founders of worldwide Presbyterianism. He had served as a chaplain to the Protestant Edward VI of England until the king's death in 1553, but left the country on the accession of the Catholic Mary I, travelling to Geneva to join Calvin's religious revolution. While there, he devised a new order of service, which was later adopted by the Church of Scotland. On his return to his homeland, he proved a steadfast opponent for Mary, Queen of Scots, rebuffing her every effort (including breaking down in tears) to co-opt him to the cause of a religious tolerance that would embrace both her own Catholicism and his Presbyterianism. An implacable, unbending man, he died in 1572 a celebrated national figure, but penniless, leaving as his legacy the conviction that religious freedom was more important than loyalty to any monarch.

1571	1646	1707
First synod of Dutch Reformed Church	Westminster Confessions	Act of Union endorses Scotland's national church

Presbyterianism also thrived in the Dutch Republic. In 1571, the Dutch Reformed Church (DRC) held its first synod at Emden and formally adopted a Calvinist programme. For a period all state officials were required to be members of the DRC, but it never became the country's established church.

Calvin's influence was felt in England too. The Westminster Confession, agreed in 1646 at a gathering of those opposing King Charles I in the English Civil War, was strongly Calvinist in its theology. It remains one of the key texts of Presbyterianism in the English-speaking world. In 1972 the English Presbyterian Church joined with the Congregationalist Church to form the United Reform Church or URC.

The Iona community

In the late 1930s, George MacLeod, a prominent Church of Scotland minister, established the Iona community on an isolated island off the west coast of Scotland from where, in the sixth century, St Columba had brought a distinctively Celtic form of Christianity to the peoples of Scotland and northern England. Over the years MacLeod faced extensive opposition from the General Assembly of his own conservative church, but he was determined to proceed with an initiative that he felt would renew Presbyterianism. The result – an ecumenical community with a distinctive liturgical approach, simple, dignified and contemporary, in the spirit of Calvin – has won admiration from all around the world.

❝Elder is identical with bishop, and before parties multiplied under diabolical influence, churches were governed by a council of elders.❞

St Jerome, 347–420

> **For anyone to arrive at God the Creator he needs Scripture as his Guide and Teacher.**
>
> John Calvin, 1559

Book of Order Presbyterian churches are confessional in that they adhere to a basic set of written texts. They share a common regard for the Book of Order as the means of regulating their practice and forms of worship. This is based on *The Form of Prayer and Ministration of the Sacraments*, first published in Geneva in 1556, an account of how congregations lived out Calvin's teachings there. In addition, Calvin's magnum opus, his *Institutes of Christian Religion*, begun in 1536 and completed in 1559, remains influential.

Most branches of the Presbyterian church continue to follow a democratic structure in line with Calvin's principles, developed in the progressive political culture of sixteenth-century Switzerland. In Scotland, local 'kirk' sessions have considerable autonomy. Above these in the hierarchy are the regional 'presbyteries' and, as the final authority, a General Assembly of lay and clerical delegates.

The Presbyterian church encourages individuals to develop their own personal relationship with God and the Bible. However, it also maintains – unlike, for example, the Baptists – that the group and the church have an equally important role in shaping belief.

the condensed idea
Religious liberty is supreme

20 Sects and cults

Originally there was just one Christian church. Unity was an overriding concern, and for a thousand years this was sufficient to hold the Church together. With the Reformation began a process of fragmentation that continues to this day. The disputes that caused the establishment of new or breakaway churches were seen in their day as profound and irreconcilable, but now they can appear minor compared with the common ground between the denominations. From the twentieth century onwards, strenuous efforts have been made at ecumenism – promoting reconciliation and reunion between the various churches – but Christian history continues to accommodate a number of numerically small but distinct groupings.

The Plymouth Brethren The original Protestants rejected Roman Christianity on the grounds of its attachment to worldly power and riches. As each of the Protestant denominations that grew out of the Reformation became more established, however, a fresh minority would object to its loss of radicalism and biblical authenticity. Such was the origin of the Plymouth Brethren in the 1820s. Disillusioned at the worldliness of their Nonconformist churches, members were attracted to a movement that began in Dublin, but which established its largest base in the English port of Plymouth. Spiritually elitist, exacting over Bible study, and rejecting all ornament, the Plymouth Brethren eschewed even displaying the cross in their meeting halls. No instruments could accompany singing, and women were required to shave or cover their heads. The Brethren believed that they were reviving the spirit of holy,

timeline

1652	1820s	1830
First Quaker meeting	Plymouth Brethren gather	Book of Mormon published

> ❝The three "S's" best expressed the way in which the Army administered to the "down and outs": first, soup; second, soap; and finally, salvation.❞

William Booth, 1829–1912

pure fellowship that had existed among the original apostles. The movement has suffered many divisions since, notably over who to admit and who to exclude. There are an estimated 2.9 million Brethren worldwide.

The Quakers George Fox (1624–91), an apprentice shoemaker from Leicestershire, founded the Society of Friends (better known as the Quakers) in 1652, after he had despaired of finding God in any existing denomination. His new movement was an association rather than a church, and was dedicated to revealing an inner truth or light. The Society has no ministers and no sacraments. Meetings are conducted largely in prayerful silence, with participants 'waiting upon God' and speaking only when prompted by the Holy Spirit. Quakers are notable for their work for social justice, especially in prisons. There are 300,000 members of the movement worldwide.

The Salvation Army Founded in 1878 by William Booth, a former Methodist minister, and his wife Catherine, the Salvation Army rejects the rituals of mainstream Christianity in favour of a simple living-out of the faith in the most trying of situations. In late Victorian Britain it was regularly attacked and ridiculed as the 'Skeleton Army', but it has grown to attract widespread admiration for its charitable work, if not a rush of converts. Its mission is characterized by outdoor evangelism, complete with brass bands, and a quasi-military organization and dress code. It meets in citadels rather

1875	1878	1884
Mary Baker Eddy's *Science and Health*	Salvation Army summoned	Jehovah's Witnesses founded

Ellen White

Although in her lifetime Ellen White (1827–1915) rejected the label of prophet, her many admirers in the Seventh-Day Adventist Church and beyond find Christian inspiration in her accounts of her visions. In one of the best known of these, White saw an 'Advent people' being guided along a dangerous path by the light of Christ towards a 'new Jerusalem'. She was a prolific writer as well as a preacher, and her 40 devotional works have made her the most widely translated non-fiction female author in history. Her subjects included her own beliefs, mysticism, health and lifestyles (she was a keen advocate of vegetarianism). Originally a Methodist, she found a ready audience for her output in the 1860s in the Sabbatarian Adventists, the movement that grew to become the Seventh-Day Adventists, and among whose membership her writings now have the status of holy books.

than churches and dedicates itself to social action with the most needy sections of the community – drug users, the homeless and prostitutes. It has no sacraments and sees every meal as a re-creation of Jesus's Last Supper. There are 2.6 million members in 118 countries around the globe.

Christian Scientists In her 1875 book *Science and Health*, Mary Baker Eddy described how she suffered half a century of ill health before she was cured by placing her faith completely in God. Her followers, known as Christian Scientists, endorse her conviction that humans are spiritual rather than physical beings and therefore her belief that God, not medicines and doctors, is the key to being healed of worldly maladies. Baker Eddy founded the First Church of Christ, Scientist, in Boston, and there are today some 1,800 branches of the Christian Scientist movement around the world.

Millennialists Millennialist movements within Christianity preach that the end of the world is nigh. They take as their inspiration the final book of the Bible, Revelation, which prophesies the second coming of Jesus to rule over an earthly paradise for a thousand years. The Jehovah's Witnesses, founded in 1884 and claiming a following of seven million worldwide, believe this will happen imminently. They are best known for their doorstep evangelism but otherwise tend to shun the rest of society in favour of fellow Witnesses. Seventh-Day Adventists, another millennialist group, engage by contrast in much social activity,

The Book of Revelation

The Book of Revelation, also called the Book of the Apocalypse, tells of an extraordinary and vivid battle in heaven between God and Satan. It has contributed significantly to both fear of the Devil and millennialist speculation within Christianity. Some believe that the book's authors, in around CE 100, were creating an allegory about the suffering of the Jews under the 'evil' overlordship of the Roman Empire, but many Christians have taken literally its talk of the beast 666, dragons, serpents, the four horsemen of the apocalypse and a final Armageddon. The closing promise of Revelation is that God will triumph over evil. Jesus will return, banish Satan and initiate a thousand years of messianic rule on earth.

especially in the field of health care. They number around 14 million, pay special regard to the prophecies of the American visionary Ellen White, and believe that the Lord's Day should be marked on Saturday rather than Sunday.

Mormons Another nineteeth-century breakaway movement within Christianity was Joseph Smith's Church of Jesus Christ of Latter-Day Saints, which today has 12 million members worldwide, with its headquarters in Salt Lake City. They are better known as the Mormons, so called because they use the Book of Mormon alongside the Bible in teaching and study. They believe that this tells the story of God's dealings with the ancient inhabitants of the American continent, including a visit to them by the risen Jesus. The movement maintains that Mormon was an American prophet who compiled the history of the ancient civilization from old records and inscribed it on plates of gold, which Smith discovered in 1823 buried in New York State. He published their contents in 1830. For Mormons, this is the unaltered word of God.

the condensed idea
There are many ways to follow Christ

21 Rapture

A distinctive feature of the latter part of the twentieth century, especially in the United States, was the rise of a new type of Christian fundamentalism. It was no longer considered enough to join a denomination. To be a true believer, you had to be 'born again' in Christ. Hand-in-hand with this insistence came healing services, the casting out of devils, TV evangelists, the elaborate theory of Dispensationalism, and a concept called rapture, which suggested that with the end of the world looming, Christians would be beamed up to heaven like characters in the popular TV series *Star Trek*.

The phrase 'born again' comes from John's gospel, in which Jesus says that those who are born again will see heaven. It began to be used widely in the 1960s, particularly in the United States, as part of a wider Evangelical revival, and referred specifically to a spiritual rebirth, a fresh or renewed acceptance of Jesus Christ into individual lives. Many born-again Christians belong to independent or semi-independent churches, including the 'house-church' movement, which has loose connections with the Baptists; and indeed, members of this movement often undergo baptism by total immersion.

Charismatic spirit This new breed of free-standing churches favours an uninhibited style of worship, drawing on Pentecostalism and the charismatic movement, another 1960s revival, which places great emphasis on being open to the gifts of the Holy Spirit. Other features of born-again services include hell-fire oratory, exorcisms and healing.

timeline

1820s	1950s
J.N. Darby plots dispensations	First TV evangelists

Televangelism

In the twentieth century, Christianity grew adept at using modern means of communication to get its message over to large congregations, as once it had used the pulpits of churches or the soapboxes of travelling preachers. It adapted first to radio, and then, in the 1950s, to television. The American Catholic bishop Fulton Sheen drew TV audiences of 30 million (and Emmy awards) for his homespun on-screen theological chats. However, it was mainly Protestant preachers who thrived thereafter in the medium, the most notable of these being the Southern Baptist Billy Graham. In the 1980s, televangelism descended into scandal over financial and sexual irregularities that saw popular hosts such as Jim and Tammy Faye Bakker and Jimmy Swaggart exposed and exiled from the airwaves.

Rapture grew out of a very particular reading, by some of these Evangelicals and fundamentalists, of St Paul's prediction, in his first letter to the Thessalonians in the New Testament, that when God descends on the earth in judgement at the end of the world, 'those who have died in Christ will be the first to rise and then those of us who are still alive will be taken up in the clouds, together with them, to meet the Lord in the air'. This was interpreted as a promise that while the rest of the world is engulfed in a time of 'Tribulation', the Armageddon predicted in the Book of Revelation, the chosen few, or 'born again', will be spared by being 'raptured' out of the conflict zone and up to heaven. This rescue will last for a set period of time, sometimes estimated at seven years, before a return to a cleaned-up earth, which will be ruled by Jesus from Jerusalem for a thousand years.

This theory contradicts every other Christian tenet, but has proved disarmingly popular. One key exponent of rapture is the former

> **‘I just want to lobby for God.’**
> **Billy Graham, 1918–**

Mississippi tub-boat captain turned leading Christian fundamentalist, Hal Lindsey. His book *The Late, Great Planet Earth* has sold 35 million copies worldwide since it was first published in 1970.

Rapture was also enthusiastically preached by the Reverend Jerry Falwell (1933–2007). Falwell, a prominent Christian fundamentalist attached to the Southern Baptist Convention, established the Moral Majority political lobbying organization, which is linked with Republican Party policies. 'You'll be riding along in an automobile,' he predicted, 'and when the trumpet sounds you and other born-again believers in that automobile will be instantly caught away – you will disappear, leaving behind only your clothes … unsaved person or persons in the automobile will be suddenly startled to find the car moving along without a driver.'

Dispensationalism Rapture is more broadly linked with an Evangelical school of thought called Dispensationalism, which dates back to the nineteenth century and the writings of the Anglo-Irish Evangelical John Nelson Darby (1800–82). Darby was one of the founders of the Plymouth Brethren, though later he split off to found the Exclusive Brethren.

The church of Scientology

There is, some critics have suggested, a science-fiction element to the concept of rapture. That same element is even more marked in the Church of Scientology, an eight-million-strong organization – some would say a cult – founded in 1953 by the sci-fi writer L. Ron Hubbard. It stands outside the Christian family, and its beliefs are based on Hubbard's own self-help system, known as Dianetics. It teaches that humans are immortal spirit beings – or thetans – who have lost their connection to God and to the wider cosmos. Scientology aims to re-establish this connection. The group is notable for its high-profile members, who include the actors Tom Cruise and John Travolta.

> 6 **Without benefit of science, space suits, or interplanetary rockets, there will be those who will be transported into a glorious place more beautiful, more awesome, than we can possibly comprehend.** 9
>
> **Hal Lindsey**

Dispensationalists divide the history of humankind – as told in the Bible – into a series of 'dispensations' or periods, each of which is characterized by God acting towards humanity in a particular way. The theory relies on a very particular and narrow reading of scripture – rejected by the vast majority of Christians and denominations – which is often called literalist, but which in fact requires a great deal of imagination. The seven dispensations are: (1) Innocence (prior to Adam and Eve's fall in the Garden of Eden); (2) Conscience (from Adam to Noah); (3) Government (from Noah to Abraham); (4) Promise (from Abraham to Moses); (5) Law (from Moses to Christ); (6) Church or Grace (currently); and (7) Kingdom (the end times that are soon to begin).

Darby's original speculation has been revived and promoted most notably by the Dispensationalists' current spiritual home, the Dallas Theological Seminary in Texas. Among more contemporary readings of the theory is the suggestion that the establishment of the state of Israel in 1948 was the first stage in the build-up to the end of the world, as predicted by Revelation. Indeed, the Dispensationalists maintain that the whole recent history of the Middle East is contained in Revelation, and that the world is moving slowly but inexorably towards a third and final world war, which will start in that region.

the condensed idea
The second coming is nigh

22 Being Jewish

**Judaism is the oldest of the three monotheistic creeds, but
with 16 million followers it is also the smallest. It epitomizes
the ancient view that religion is not so much about believing as
doing. A central term in Judaism is *emunah* – faith – which
encapsulates not just the idea of putting your trust in God, but
also all that follows from that, in terms of living your life
according to moral, God-given principles.**

There is no word in Hebrew for Judaism. Indeed, some scholars argue
that the term only came into use as late as the nineteenth century. You
can be a Jew without subscribing to all, or any, of the tenets of Judaism
as set out in the Jewish Law and defined by rabbis. All you need is a
Jewish mother. So 'secular' Jews may accept Jewish values and some of
its traditional practices, but will not attribute a religious significance to
them. Rather they see Jewishness as a sign of cultural and ethnic
identity. This combination of religion and race in Judaism is different
from anything found in other faiths.

Chosen people The sacred writings of Judaism are the Jewish Bible,
which includes the books of the Torah (Genesis, Exodus, Leviticus,
Numbers and Deuteronomy) but not those of the New Testament; the
Talmud (rabbinic writings); and the *siddur*, or prayer book. Key to the
history of the Jewish people as narrated in the Torah is God's promise in
Exodus that the Jews are his chosen people: 'If you obey my voice and
hold fast to my covenant, you of all nations shall be my very own for all
the Earth is mine. I will count you a kingdom of priests, a consecrated
nation.' How to interpret that promise – and the rest of the Bible – was

timeline

c.1200 BCE	586 BCE	70 CE	c.600
Start of Jewish kingdom	Babylonian exile	Second Temple destroyed	Talmud completed

principally the task of rabbis (or teachers). Their commentaries, or Mishnah, many of them spoken rather than written, were first collected in print around 200 CE. They then went through various revisions, adjusting to new and specific circumstances, before emerging around 600 CE as what is known as the Talmud (from the Hebrew 'to learn').

The experience of exile Jewish history spans 3,500 years – more than three quarters of the history of civilized humanity – and begins, according to the Torah, with the Patriarch Abraham. The Jews were chosen by God as a special people to set an example of holiness. God guided them out of Egypt and enabled them to defeat their enemies and set up their own homeland around 1200 BCE. On Mount Sinai, he gave Moses, the most important prophet in Judaism, a set of rules for living an ethical life, known as the Ten Commandments.

> 'Am I a Jew by religion, by people, by tribe, by nationality, by race?'
>
> Rabbi Julia Neuberger, 1995

Maimonides' 13 principles

The twelfth century saw an enduringly popular attempt to summarize the essence of Judaism. The scholar and philosopher Maimonides (Rabbi Moses Ben Maimon) laid down 13 principles: God exists; God is one; God is not in bodily form; God is eternal; Jews must worship him alone; God has communicated through the prophets; Moses is the greatest of the prophets; the Torah is of divine origin; the Torah is eternally valid; God knows the deeds of human beings; God punishes the evil and rewards the good; God will send a Messiah; and God will resurrect the dead.

c.1800	c.1900	1939	1948
Orthodox/Reform spilt	Liberal movement	Nazi Holocaust	State of Israel

> **The Jews created a separate and specific identity earlier than almost any other people which survives to this day.**
> **Paul Johnson, 1987**

The Jewish kingdom thrived. In 960 BCE, King Solomon built a great Temple in Jerusalem, which became the focus of rites and rituals. It was destroyed in 586 BCE by the Babylonians, who exploited divisions between the Jews to defeat them. Many Jews were carried off to exile, the first of several such occurrences in Jewish history. Restored to Israel, a new kingdom existed until the first century CE, in its later years under resented Roman overlordship. A revolt led to the destruction of a second Temple in 70 CE. From this time onwards there was a drive to set down the Jewish tradition in writing.

Persecution of the Jews increased as they travelled far and wide throughout Europe, though they found a particular haven in Spain under its Islamic rulers around 1000 CE. Thereafter they experienced ever greater restrictions in Christian Europe until, in the early years of the nineteenth century, a new age of liberty brought them freedoms in the West and beyond (the first Jews arrived in America in 1648) but continuing persecution in the East. The Nazi Holocaust of the first half of the 1940s left six million Jews dead as Hitler attempted to eliminate a whole people. In 1948, the Jews were granted their own homeland with the founding of the state of Israel.

Orthodox, Reform and Liberal From the seventh to the nineteenth centuries, the Jewish people largely avoided labels and stressed what they had in common – exile or *galut* from the promised land. However, the emancipation that characterized society in the 1800s saw the adoption of terms to categorize Jewish belief that remain familiar to this day. Those who laid the heaviest emphasis on tradition and the law called themselves simply Observant but were described by others as Orthodox. They constitute around 10–15 per cent of Jews today. Reform Judaism emerged from a re-evaluation of traditional Judaism in the light of changing circumstances in nineteenth-century Europe. Old rules dating back almost 2,000 years were abandoned (for instance those relating to the privileges of a priestly caste of families, and the requirements of ritual purity). The Reform movement embraces the largest proportion of modern believing Jews. The Liberal movement began as an offshoot of the Reform grouping at the start of the twentieth century. It has further updated various aspects of the faith, regarding as Jewish anyone with a Jewish parent (rather than only a Jewish mother) and appointing women as rabbis. Its aim is to reconcile traditional Judaism with the modern world.

Ultra-Orthodoxy

Of the several strands of Ultra-Orthodoxy in modern Judaism, the most prominent is Hasidism, a name that comes from the Hebrew *hasid* or 'pious'. The term was first used in the second century BCE of especially devout Jews, and was revived in Eastern Europe in the eighteenth century among oppressed Jewish peasants in places such as Poland and Lithuania. The movement aimed to deepen devotion, often through music and mysticism, and stressed spirituality rather than scholarship. It was carried to Western Europe and beyond by waves of emigration. Modern Hasidic communities are tight-knit and insist on strict rules of modesty. Men sport long locks of hair under their ears in response to the demand in Leviticus not to trim the edges of beards.

the condensed idea
Jews are God's chosen people

23 Jewish rites of passage

The distinctive collection of rites and rituals of Judaism, developed over 3,500 years, continues to give shape to the lives of Jews. Its origins are found, as with everything else in the faith, in the Hebrew Bible and the covenant it describes between God and his chosen people. The endurance of these rituals owes much to the desire of the Jewish people to maintain their identity during long periods of exile and persecution. They have become part of what it is to be Jewish today, though the extent to which they are observed often depends on the type of Judaism embraced by each individual.

The very first obligation – or *mitzvah* – that the Torah places on Jews comes in Chapter 1 of the Book of Genesis, namely to 'be fruitful and multiply'. Having children is a religious requirement for Jews, bringing new life to that central relationship with God and thus strengthening his rule on Earth. It has also served the practical purpose of keeping up the numbers in what is by far the smallest of the three monotheistic religions. Hasidic Jews, in particular, take the duty seriously.

Judaism upholds the sanctity of human life and objects to contraceptives, though it grades them on a scale from the least objectionable (oral devices such as pills, whose earliest forms are

timeline

1200 BCE
Rules of Jewish life laid down in Torah

1800s
Reform questions kosher rules

described in rabbinic literature) to the most (condoms or withdrawal). These judgements are made by comparing the various methods with the injunction in the Book of Genesis against 'spilling the seed'. Abortion does not carry in Judaism the same prohibition as found in Catholicism, and is encouraged if the mother's life is in danger.

Ceremonies In accordance with God's wishes, as set out in the Torah, all male Jewish children make a covenant 'in the flesh' when they are eight days old by undergoing circumcision – having their foreskin removed. It is, Jews believe, a physical mark of their commitment to God. According to the Torah, the operation should be carried out by the father of the infant, but most appoint a *mohel* – usually a specially trained rabbi and/or doctor – to do the procedure for them. It used to take place in the synagogue but is now more usually performed in the family home. Both newborn male and female children are named and blessed in synagogue rituals. Circumcision is also demanded of male converts to Judaism.

What is Kosher?

Jewish dietary laws have their origin in the Hebrew Bible and are known as *kashrut*, from which derives the word *kosher* to describe what can be eaten. Sometimes thought of as relating to health and hygiene, these rules are more fundamentally to do with holiness and doing what the Bible says, however irrational it may seem to contemporary minds. Maimonides described the dietary laws as 'training us to master our appetites, accustom us to restrain our desires, and avoid considering the pleasure of eating and drinking as the goal of man's existence'. Orthodox Jews follow the exacting laws carefully – including separating meat and milk, declining fish if it doesn't have fins and scales, and slaughtering meat in a prescribed way. Some even follow the decree in Leviticus that fruit should not be eaten from a tree that is less than three years old. This strict observance is another factor in setting Orthodox Jews apart from the world. Reform Jews in the nineteenth century argued that *kashrut* had become an end in itself and served only to distance Jews from non-Jews. Today, many Reform and Liberal Jews keep or discard the rules according to their own personal preference.

> **❝God said to Abraham ... "All your males must be circumcised. You shall circumcise your foreskin and this shall be the sign of the Covenant between myself and you."❞**
>
> Genesis **17:11–12**

According to the Talmud, coming of age happens at the age of 13. This is when young Jews are regarded as able to fulfil the commandments. A Jewish boy becomes Bar Mitzvah and a Jewish girl Bat Mitzvah – 'sons and daughters of the commandment'. The Reform tradition marks both occasions with ceremonies, regarding male and female as equal before God.

Although the traditional injunction in Judaism against 'marrying out' – in other words, marrying a non-Jew – goes against modern ideas of individual liberty and religious toleration, it is understandable, in historical terms, as part of a determination in exile and under persecution to maintain a homogeneous community. The injunction is still widely followed in Orthodox and Ultra-Orthodox circles – where strict adherence in the home to dietary and ritual purity laws would make it difficult to maintain a 'mixed' household. In Reform and Liberal branches, marrying out is tolerated but remains a cause of anguish for many parents. Though they welcome the integration of their Jewish children into broader society, and appreciate that mixed marriages reduce anti-Semitism, they cannot help but regret the dilution of Jewish identity. In the United States, over 50 per cent of Jews marry out.

Unlike Christianity, Judaism is not a missionary religion. It does not actively go out to seek converts. If they present themselves, it carefully scrutinizes their wish to convert, and can and does say no.

Hebrew calendar The Hebrew calendar is a complex and crowded one. An ancient faith such as Judaism has a strong sense of the passage of time, and this is seen in the daily pattern of prayer and the separation of *Shabbat* (the Sabbath, marked on a Saturday) from the rest of the week. With the exception of the Day of Atonement, all the special days

Zionism

The connection between Judaism and Zionism is a close one, but the two should not be seen as the same thing. Zionism, in modern terms at least, is a political and nationalistic movement that from the 1880s onwards promoted the right of the Jewish people to a state of their own in Palestine, site of God's original covenant with their ancestors. In 1917, pressure from Zionists led to the Balfour Declaration, in which the British, who then governed Palestine, endorsed the idea of a Jewish homeland. Concern about the fate of those non-Jews already living in Palestine grew as the area subsequently became a focus for Jewish immigration from all around the world. Following the Nazi Holocaust, and a terrorist campaign against the British forces in Palestine, the state of Israel was established in 1948. Forty per cent of the world's Jews now live there, but many people from all strands of Judaism question the achievements of Zionism. The Ultra-Orthodox Jews, for example, see modern Israel as too secular – not Jewish enough – while many Liberal Jews disown the actions of the Israeli government and the settlers in occupied areas.

in the calendar recall God's presence in nature and history – especially the history of the Jewish people.

Passover, in the spring, is a period of 49 days marking the exodus of the Jewish people out of slavery in Egypt. It culminates in the festival of Shavuot, which commemorates the giving of the Torah and the Ten Commandments on Mount Sinai. Balancing this in the autumn is Rosh Hashanah, the 'New Year', followed 10 days later by Yom Kippur – 'the Day of Atonement' – and the Sukkot, or Feast of Tabernacles, which recalls the journey through the wilderness to the promised land under God's protection.

the condensed idea
There's a distinct Jewish way of life

24 Kabbalah

Within all three of the monotheistic religions there are those who advocate a more mystical, imaginative and intuitive approach to belief. In Judaism, that movement is known as Kabbalah. Its key text, the Sefer-ha-Zohar (or 'brightness'), first appeared in Spain in the 1280s, but its devotees claim the book represents a hidden erotic spiritual tradition within Judaism that dates back to the first century CE and beyond. It has reinvigorated the prayer and spiritual life of many Jews, and helped them to discover a meaning to their faith that goes beyond its rules, rites and rituals. However, others in mainstream Judaism regard modern manifestations of Kabbalah as superstitious and overly concerned with visions of evil spirits.

The Zohar was written or compiled in 1280 by a Spanish rabbi, Moses de Leon (c.1250–1305). He claimed to be working from a much earlier text by Rabbi Shimon bar Yohai, a prominent teacher around 70 CE when the second Temple in Jerusalem was destroyed. How he had come about the text was never made clear. The ancient document, a collection of Shimon bar Yohai's oral commentaries on the Torah, had, according to de Leon, subsequently been left out of the Talmud and lost or concealed.

There has been much debate about Moses de Leon's claims for the Zohar. The text contains references to events that happened well after 70 CE. Believers maintain that these prove that Shimon bar Yohai was a prophet. Some even claim that he predicted that his writings would be concealed for 1,200 years before miraculously reappearing to guide the Jews.

However, it is widely reported that after de Leon's death, his impoverished widow responded to an offer to purchase the original text from which he had worked by saying that no such document had ever existed. Her husband had simply made it up. Devotees of the Zohar hold that the book's words were produced under divine influence.

Sefirot

The *sefirot* in Kabbalah are the ten 'emanations' of God with which he creates the universe. They correspond to various levels of creation, or branches on the tree of life, and are the means by which God progressively reveals himself and his ethical principles to his people. They are *keter* (will); *chochmah* (wisdom); *binah* (understanding); *chesed* (mercy); *gevurah* (justice); *tiferet* (harmony); *netzach* (victory); *hod* (glory); *yesod* (power); and *malkuth* (kingdom).

Inner meaning In its examination of the Torah, the Zohar describes four levels of interpretation – literal, allegorical, that guided by rabbinic teaching, and finally an inner response, or *sod*. The initials in Aramaic (the ancient language used by Moses de Leon) of these four levels together spell a word that means 'orchard' or 'paradise'. In searching for inner meaning, the Zohar preaches, Jews must engage with God's love in obedience and prayer by embarking on a spiritual journey that will be marked by holy visions and measured out in seven colour-coded stages of ecstasy. The final stage will be colourless as the believer contemplates the dazzling mystery of God.

> **❝[Kabbalah] frightens people, so they try to denigrate it or trivialize it, so that it makes more sense.❞**
> **Madonna, 2005**

1480s
Jews expelled from Spain

c.1500
Isaac Luria refines Kabbalah

Overall there is an erotic tone to the Zohar's descriptions of humankind's relationship with both God and the Torah, so much so that in the seventeenth century there was a move to restrict access to the Zohar to men over the age of 40.

Unknowable God The main tenets of religion presented in the Zohar are broadly empowering of humanity. The good man or woman can, it claims, enhance the universe by their actions and so prompt an outpouring of divine grace. This remains one of the principal propositions of the broader Kabbalah movement, which seeks to make a connection between an infinite and eternal creator God and those individuals who populate his finite creation.

Kabbalah consists of ways to attain spiritual self-realization. These include prayer, reflection, and commitment to a mystical journey that will reconcile the external practice of religion (Jewish rites and rituals) with its inner meaning. It is, however, a broader theological and mystical system than just the Zohar. Its adherents would argue that it dates back to the tenth century BCE, when it was the norm for the Jewish people living in ancient Israel. It was only during subsequent upheavals, battles, exile and sufferings, they claim, that it became buried or hidden.

In the Talmud, the word *kabbalah* simply means 'received knowledge', but over the centuries that followed the wide dissemination of the Zohar among medieval Jewry, the mystical principles it outlined entered the mainstream of Jewish theological thinking. This process was

> **More valuable than the garment is the body which carries it, and more valuable even than that is the soul which animates the body. Fools see only the garment of the Torah, the more intelligent see the body, the wise see the soul, its proper being; and in the Messianic time the "upper soul" of the Torah will stand revealed.**
>
> **Zohar**

Madonna and Kabbalah

Though raised as a Catholic, the singer Madonna became a prominent devotee of Kabbalah after being introduced to it in 1997 by her friend, the actress and comedian Sandra Bernhard. She credits it with enabling her to find a greater sense of self-worth and spiritual direction. As part of her connection, she adopted a Hebrew name, Esther, and wore in public a red Kabbalah wristband, knotted seven times, said to ward off evil spirits. She follows a particular form of Kabbalah promoted by Rabbi Philip Berg, who has established 50 Kabbalah centres worldwide since founding his first in Jerusalem in 1969. On her 1998 album *Ray of Light* Madonna credited the Kabbalah Centre for its 'creative guidance', and in the children's book she published in 2003 she reflected the movement's moral disapproval of greed and envy.

accelerated by the destruction and scattering of the Jewish community in Spain from the 1490s onwards. In the process, Kabbalah moved from something academic, the preserve of upper-class Jews, to a popular movement, with kabbalistic anthologies circulating throughout the Jewish diaspora, prescribing an esoteric route for direct communion with God.

Kabbalah became the subject of many debates and revisions, most notably by Isaac Luria (1534–72) in his school of kabbalistic studies at Safed in northern Galilee. Lurianic Kabbalah places special emphasis on the cosmos, meditation, and the coming of a Jewish Messiah. It makes a clear distinction between Ein Sof – that aspect of God that will forever be unknowable because it is endless and impersonal – and the *sefirot*, the ten revealed aspects, that shape the lives of Jews, the fate of Israel and human history.

the condensed idea
The mystery of God can be partially unravelled

25 Anti-Semitism

All religions and religious believers have at some point in history faced prejudice, from either secular rulers, fellow citizens or followers of other creeds. The Jews, however, have experienced this for longer and in more extreme forms than anyone else. From the anti-Jewish riots in Alexandria in the third century BCE through to the Nazi Holocaust from 1939 to 1945, which killed six million Jews, the shadow of anti-Semitism has defined Jewish identity.

Hostility towards the Jews existed long before Christianity came along. The Greeks and Romans both attacked the Jewish people in their midst, accusing them of exaggerated influence, overblown financial control and strange hidden practices, an echo of every charge that was later to be laid in Christian Europe. But the breaking away of the Christian Church from Judaism in the first century CE bequeathed a legacy of particular hatred and suspicion between the two that was only put aside as recently as 1965, when the Vatican formally absolved the Jews of the crime of deicide – killing God.

The Devil's refuge The leaders of the early Church, anxious to make a clear distinction between themselves and their Jewish roots, stopped at nothing in their condemnation of Judaism. St John Chrysostom (c.344–407), in a series of eight sermons to the people of Antioch in 387, provided all the weapons used by succeeding generations, maintaining that the Jews were carnal, lascivious, avaricious, accursed and demonic. They had murdered all the prophets, then crucified Christ, and they worshipped the Devil. St Jerome

3rd century BCE
Anti-Jewish riots in Alexandria

1st century CE
First 'blood libel'

(c.340–420) labelled the synagogue 'a brothel, a den of vice, the Devil's refuge, Satan's fortress, a place to deprave the soul, an abyss of every conceivable disaster and whatever else you will'. The first record of a synagogue being burnt down by Christians comes in 338 at Callicnicul on the Euphrates.

> **The Jew is the very devil incarnal.**
>
> **William Shakespeare,** *c.*1596

The demonization of the Jews by Christians was exceptionally vicious. Jews were readily equated with the Devil, Jesus's adversary in the New Testament. They were accused of carrying his mark and doing his work. One popular notion in medieval Christianity was the so-called *foetor judaicus*, the foul sulphur smell given off by Jews that was also a sign of the Devil. Another accusation was that Jews kidnapped Christian children to offer their blood as a sacrifice to the Devil. In medieval Christian art, the Devil was often depicted as having a long, hooked nose, supposedly a physical characteristic he shared with the Jews.

Blood libel

Blood libels – false accusations that a particular group, usually religious, is carrying out rituals using the blood of their victims – have been recorded since the first century CE, when the Greek chronicler Apion accused the Jews of sacrificing captured Greeks as part of ceremonies in the Jerusalem Temple. Christians faced the same charge in the next century when their Roman persecutors distorted the symbolism of Jesus's body and blood in the bread and wine of the Eucharist to claim that the fledgling Church was drinking blood at its services. The first Christian blood libel against the Jews came in 1144, when the Jews of Norwich were accused of capturing, killing and sacrificing a delivery boy. The charges were rejected by a court, but the accused Jews had to escape a lynch mob. The Church later made the boy, William of Norwich, into a saint.

338
First record of synagogue burnt by Christians

1144
Murder of William of Norwich

1939–45
Nazi Holocausts

1965
Vatican clears Jews of deicide

Scapegoating Though the given reason for much of the Christian hostility to the Jews was their alleged crime of deicide – killing Jesus – the real reasons were often more practical. In medieval Europe, a tiny minority of Jews (no more than 1.5 million across the continent) were often over-represented in the professions of law, medicine and finance. Their disproportionate success made them the focus of envy and scapegoating. When a king or a prince needed someone to blame for things going wrong in his kingdom, the Jews were an easy target. In 1750, when Empress Maria Theresa of Austria, a devout Christian woman, needed to raise some extra revenue, she first banned Jews

Pope Pius XII and the Jews

Pius XII was elected Pope in 1939, months before the outbreak of the Second World War. He stands accused by Jewish historians of anti-Semitism because of his decision to remain silent throughout the war years about the Nazi Holocaust, even though he knew what was happening. His critics say that he turned a blind eye to Nazi atrocities because he feared that Hitler was the only alternative to Soviet-style communism sweeping across Europe and destroying the Church. It is further charged that Vatican diplomats failed to help Jews escape persecution by getting visas to travel to Palestine because the Pope opposed the idea of a Jewish homeland there. In the immediate post-war period, it is claimed, Pius showed his true colours by allowing the Vatican to be used as a conduit to spirit Nazi war criminals away to Africa and Latin America. His defenders counter that he was not anti-Semitic, that he was unaware of the true horror of the Holocaust, and that he believed (erroneously) that he had to maintain a stance of strict neutrality so as to maintain the independence of the Church and play a part in the eventual peace settlement. In 1999, the Vatican agreed to establish a joint commission with Jewish historians to research its own archives and present a fuller picture of Pius's role. Two years later, the Jewish members of the committee stood down in protest at Rome's refusal to open its archive fully.

> ❝The Christian demonising of the Jews goes right back to the Jewish rejection of Jesus – the old question of the Jews having killed Jesus. In that the image of the Jews as demons was made.❞
>
> **Rabbi Norman Solomon, 1933–**

from the Bohemian lands of her far-flung domains, then allowed then back in on condition they paid her a special tax for the privilege once every ten years.

Christians were not alone in attacking the Jews. In the eighteenth century, various great Enlightenment thinkers such as Voltaire, defenders of conscience and liberty in every other regard, vilified them for their greed, avarice and even for their habit of marking the Sabbath. In nineteenth-century Germany, scientists prepared supposedly learned papers purporting to prove the inferiority of the Jewish people.

Islamic tolerance Islam has traditionally been much more tolerant than Christianity of Jews, perhaps because the two faiths, while sharing a monotheistic approach, are not such close relatives as Judaism and Christianity. From the ninth century through to the nineteenth, Jews often enjoyed greater religious liberty in Muslim lands than in Christian ones, though it was the pogroms against them in eleventh-century Spain, hitherto a place of tolerance and mutual respect between Islamic rulers and Jewish subjects, that sent many Jews to a new place of exile in Christian Europe. In the twentieth century, and especially after the establishment of the state of Israel in 1948 on land that had previously belonged to mainly Muslim Palestinians, some in Islam became notably less tolerant of Judaism.

the condensed idea
Anti-semitism is the oldest prejudice

26 The birth of Islam

The story of the growth of Islam is a remarkable one. In 610 CE, the Prophet Muhammad received the word of God on a lonely mountaintop just outside the holy city of Mecca in present-day Saudi Arabia. A century after his death in 632, belief in the message he had received had spread westwards along the coast of North Africa as far as Spain, and in the opposite direction all the way to the Himalayas. At first Allah's revelations to Muhammad were shared orally, but after his death they were written down as the Qur'an – a word that means 'recitation'.

Muhammad was a merchant by profession, working in Mecca. The city had grown rapidly into a major trading post, a transformation that had brought with it social tensions. It was also a religious centre, a place of pilgrimage or *hajj*, where Arabs would come to worship their various tribal gods. Though they knew of the Jewish and Christian traditions of having but one god, and felt no hostility to them, they preferred a vaguer spiritual code that gave tribal solidarity – called *muruwah* – a sacred value.

Muhammad believed that a coming together of beliefs would bring greater peace and justice. Once a year he would retreat to a cave outside Mecca to pray for guidance – and to distribute alms to the growing number of poor and marginalized in the city. In 610, when he was 40 years old, he was alone in the cave when, according to his own

timeline

570	595	610
Birth of Muhammad	Marries Khadijah	Night of Destiny

description, he was gripped by an overwhelming embrace. At first he thought he was being attacked by a djinn – or evil spirit – but it was in fact the Angel Gabriel speaking the words of a new Arabic scripture direct from God, or Allah.

Muhammad's family

Muhammad's first wife, Khadijah, was older than him and a widow of independent means when they married. Though polygamy was the norm in Arabia at the time, Muhammad took no other wife while she was alive. They had at least six children – two sons, Al-Qasim and Abdullah, who died in infancy, and four daughters, Zaynab, Ruqayyah, Umm Kulthum and Fatimah. Khadijah died in 619, in what Muhammad's early biographers call his 'year of sadness'. After that he married at least nine more times, often for political or humanitarian reasons. The homely Sawdah, for instance, another widow, was the cousin of a local tribal chief. His favourite wife, according to Sunni Muslims, was Aisha, who was only six years old when they were betrothed. After his death, she was involved in collecting his teachings in the Hadith. Another wife, Zaynab bint Jahsh, was first married to one of his adopted sons, but they divorced so Muhammad could wed her. Islam teaches that the Prophet was a helpful husband, sharing in household chores, and allowing his wives – by the standards of the time – an unusual degree of freedom. In the latter years of his life, however, his wives greeted visitors from behind a screen, and were required not to remarry should he die before them. This has subsequently been quoted as a reason why all Muslim women should wear the veil.

622	630	632
Hijrah	Defends Mecca	Death of Muhammad

After that first 'Night of Destiny', Muhammad experienced similar revelations many times, and it was often a painful process. Yet his behaviour illustrates the perfect surrender (*islam* in Arabic) that every human being should make to the divine.

Day of reckoning At first Muhammad was cautious about speaking publicly of what had happened, but as the news spread, Allah's words about inner transformation, social equality, unity, mutual respect and peace won many devotees. This was an age when ongoing war between Persia and Byzantium and between local tribes caused many in Arabia to fear for the future of humankind.

As Muhammad recited each new revelation, his followers would learn it by heart. Those who were literate wrote it down. A key message was that there was only one God, Allah, and that people would one day be called before him to account for their actions. There would be a day of reckoning – *yawn ad-din*, an Arabic term that also conveys 'moment of truth'.

Hijrah Muhammad's teaching proved unpopular, and though he was anxious to avoid confrontation at all costs, he and his followers were attacked in Mecca. There were fears Muhammad would be assassinated. At times he was close to despair, but he was strengthened by his faith in Allah and by the continuing revelations – notably a dream-like night journey when he was conveyed by Gabriel to Jerusalem. In 622, he led around 70 followers, plus their families, on a *hijrah* (migration) to Medina to escape the tensions in Mecca.

❝Never once did I receive a revelation without thinking that my soul had been torn away from me... Sometimes it comes unto me like the reverberations of a bell, and that is the hardest upon me; the reverberations abate when I am aware of their message.❞

Muhammad, 570–632

> **At that time people will straggle forth
> To be shown what they have done
> Whoever does a mote's weight good will
> see it Whoever does a mote's weight
> wrong will see it.**

Qur'an 99:6-9

The Final Sermon

Muhammad died in the arms of his wife Aisha on 8 June 632. His 'Final Sermon' was delivered shortly before his death to a gathering of 120,000 pilgrims at Mount Arafat. A summarized text of this sermon is found in mosques all around the world. In it, he instructed his hearers to abandon feuds and in-fighting and preached tolerance. 'An Arab has no superiority over a non-Arab; a white has no superiority over a black, nor a black over a white, except by piety and good deeds.'

The hostility between Muhammad and the people of Mecca finally spilt over into open warfare. Although Muhammad was not a pacifist, he did see violence as a last resort. A revelation told him not to kill those his followers took prisoner, as was the custom, but to release or ransom them. In 627 he defeated a siege at Medina by an army from Mecca. This proved to be a turning point. In 630 he returned to Mecca in triumph. His victories had united the tribes of Arabia and unleashed a wave of converts throughout the peninsula and beyond.

the condensed idea
Muhammad was God's final prophet

27 The Pillars of Islam

Islam teaches that faith must come first and that it cannot be tailored or compromised to fit round secular lives. At the heart of the commitment it demands are the 'Pillars of Islam', a concept shared by all branches of the religion. These pillars – numbers vary between the different Islamic traditions – represent the duties incumbent on every Muslim if they are to lead a good and responsible life in line with Allah's teaching. They shape the daily lives of the one-billion-plus Muslims worldwide.

Sunnis – who make up around 60 per cent of all Muslims – hold that there are five pillars. These are: (1) Shahadah – sincerely reciting the Muslim profession of faith that 'there is no God but Allah and Muhammad is the Prophet of Allah'; (2) Salat – performing five times each day, facing Mecca, the ritual prayers (dawn, noon, mid-afternoon, sunset, night); (3) Zakat – paying an alms (or charity) tax to benefit the poor and the needy; (4) Sawm – abstaining from food, drink, cigarettes and sex during daylight hours in the month of Ramadan; and (5) Hajj – making the once-in-a-lifetime pilgrimage to Mecca.

Hadith If the Qur'an sets out for Muslims the word of Allah, then the Hadith, the sayings and teachings of Muhammad, enables them to understand and imitate his life and example – which together are known in Islam as the Sunnah. While the Qur'an is roughly equivalent

timeline

c.635	c.730
Qur'an started after death of Muhammad	First written versions of Hadith

in length to the Christian New Testament, the Hadith stretches to many volumes and is much debated. After its first written versions started circulating, around a hundred years after the Prophet's death, many unauthorized texts also appeared, claiming to represent Muhammad's life. Strict rules were then established to decide which of these were authentic. The most revered remains the collection put together by Isma'il al-Bukhari (d.870 CE).

> 'Take whatever the Messenger gives you, and keep away from what he forbids you.'
>
> Qur'an 59:7

Together the Qur'an, the Hadith and the Sunnah form the basis for Islamic – or Shar'iah – law. Up until the eleventh century, debate was encouraged between scholars as to what should be

The Hadd penalties

In Shar'iah law, Hadd (plural Hudud) laws cover specific crimes – consumption of alcohol, theft, murder, adultery, slander and apostasy. Some Muslims believe that these laws come straight from the Qur'an and therefore have divine sanction. Others argue that they are particular interpretations and represent the most extreme penalty a judge can impose. The real punishment for the offender is the knowledge that he has let Allah down. Drinking alcohol can result in flogging. Theft can be punished by limb amputation. Murder is treated by some Shar'iah jurists on the basis of a life for a life. Flogging is also prescribed for adultery or any form of sexual licence, and the Qur'an recommends it for anyone who makes an accusation against a woman that can't be substantiated by four witnesses (a result, it is thought, of Muhammad's wife Aisha being falsely accused). In some Islamic societies this law has been turned round so that a woman who accuses a man of rape can be flogged if she can't find four witnesses to the crime. Finally, regarding apostasy, the Prophet rejected any compulsion in religion, though the Qur'an describes those who repudiate Islam as being under a curse.

> 'To this day, Muslims remain deeply attached to the Shar'iah, which has made them internalize the archetypal figure of Muhammad at a very deep level and, liberating him from the seventh century, has made him a living presence in their lives and a part of themselves.'
>
> Karen Armstrong, 2000

considered Shar'iah, but such flexibility was subsequently lost, though Islam continues to allow for what it calls *istihsan* – interpreting the spirit rather than the letter of the law.

Rites of passage A new baby is welcomed into the family of Islam soon after birth by having the call to prayer – used to summon worshippers to the mosque five times a day – whispered into its right ear and the command to rise and worship into its left. Circumcision of male babies – in accordance with the same injunction that Jews find in Genesis, and which makes up part of the Qur'an – takes place at seven days if the child is healthy. As soon as they are able, children start to learn by heart verses from the Qur'an, and by the age of 10 they can participate in fasting.

Marriages are often arranged by families, following the custom of centuries, though according to Muhammad's wife Aisha, the Prophet insisted that the girl must always be consulted. No one should be forced. The marriage ceremony – or *nikah* – is often a simple affair, conducted by the imam at the mosque, but the *walimah* – or wedding party – that follows is a public acknowledgement of commitment. Mixed marriages between a Muslim male and a non-Muslim female are accepted in most societies, but the other way round is regarded with less tolerance.

Though a Muslim man may take up to four wives, the Qur'an stresses that he should only do so if his first wife is not upset by it, and if the subsequent wives do not hurt her. The man must also be able to provide materially and emotionally for the wives he takes. A woman may have it written down when she marries that if her husband takes any more wives, she can divorce him. Divorce is accepted in Islam but is regarded with great sadness. The Qur'an states that there is nothing more hateful to Allah on the face of the earth.

There is one verse in the Qur'an (4:34) that does appear to allow wife-beating, but scholars point out that it is in the context of divorce proceedings where the woman has refused to listen to reason. The Prophet, it is further noted, did not use this sanction himself with any of his wives.

The Crusades and Islamophobia

Jerusalem holds a unique place in all three monotheistic traditions. For Muslims it is the third holiest city after Mecca and Medina. In 1099, Christian Crusaders sent by the Pope to defeat the Muslim 'infidel' attacked Jerusalem, massacred 30,000 of its largely Muslim inhabitants and set up a Christian kingdom. Not until 1187 were the Crusaders dislodged by Saladin, and it was the end of the thirteenth century before they were driven out of the region altogether. The image of Muslims invoked by popes and Crusaders alike in this period – as uneducated savages, intent on war, inherently violent and intolerant – may have been at odds with actual Islamic practice, but it imprinted itself in the minds of the Christian West with lasting effect.

Islamic calendar There are two principal festivals in the Islamic calendar – Eid ul-Fitr, the feast that breaks the fast at the end of the Ramadan month, and Eid ul-Adha, the feast of sacrifice that occurs during the *hajj*. Ramadan itself simply means 'the ninth month', and was marked in Arabic culture long before Muhammad. In Islam, it is a time for atonement for sins, for stepping back from the world and concentrating on religion, and for showing patience.

the condensed idea
Faith must come first for Muslims

28 Sunni and Shi'a

Within all religions there are various traditions, sects and groups, often separated from each other by disagreements that took place many centuries ago. In the 50 years following the death of the Prophet, a split appeared in Islam between the majority, the Sunni, and a radical minority, the Shi'a, who felt they were closer to the Prophet's life and example. At the same time as Islam was spreading both west and east at great speed, there was a fundamental breach at its centre. The legacy of this schism 1,300 years ago remains part of the Muslim world to this day.

When Muhammad died in 632, he had two potential successors – his cousin and son-in-law Ali ibn Abi Talib, and his first adult male convert, Abu Bakr. Muhammad's own preference was unclear. Ali had been raised in the Prophet's household, had married his daughter Fatimah, and had seemed to be anointed by Muhammad on his final *hajj*; Abu Bakr, however, father of Muhammad's wife Aisha, had been selected by the Prophet to lead prayers during his final illness.

Finally the choice was made, and Abu Bakr was named caliph – or leader. When he died two years later, he nominated his own successor, Umar ibn al-Khattab, who was caliph for 10 years, overseeing the spread of Islam to Jerusalem in 638. During this time, the Islamic caliphate replaced the Persian and Byzantine empires in the region and brought religious tolerance in its wake. Conquered peoples were given the choice of embracing Islam and avoiding taxes, or sticking to their own beliefs and paying for the privilege.

timeline

632	638	656
The Prophet dies	Jerusalem falls to Islam	Ali ibn Abi Talib disputed caliph

> **'Not a single verse of the Qur'an descended upon the Messenger of God which he did not proceed to dictate to me and make me recite.'**

Ali ibn Abi Talib, c.11th century

When Umar was assassinated by a Christian slave, a group of six of his closest advisers chose as the next caliph Uthman ibn 'Affan, who was the husband of two of the Prophet's daughters. Uthman led Islam for 12 years as it reached west across North Africa and east towards the Indus Valley and China, but he faced accusations of nepotism and was assassinated in Egypt.

Battle for leadership Ali's moment had come at last. He moved the centre of the caliphate to Kufa in Iraq, where he was opposed by Aisha, the Prophet's widow, who led an army against him, claiming that he was implicated in Uthman's death. When Aisha was defeated at the Battle of the Camel at Basra in 656 and sent to live out her days in Mecca, Muawiyyah, the governor of Damascus and a kinsman of Uthman, took up the cause against Ali. Their two armies clashed at the Battle of Siffin. Muawiyyah's soldiers put pages of the Qur'an on the points of their spears, but Ali refused to give the order to engage them and a compromise was reached. Ali was killed in 661 by extremists from his own side, known as the Kharijites (whose descendants, the 500,000-strong Ibadiyah, live today in North Africa, Oman and Zanzibar).

Ali's two sons – grandsons of the Prophet – agreed to allow Muawiyyah to be caliph if he gave them both the title of imam. Peace was restored briefly, and Muawiyyah proved an able administrator, ruling from Damascus. When he died, he passed the caliphate to his son, Yazid. Ali's sons, however, objected to the leadership being treated as if it were a hereditary possession, and one of them, Husain, rose up in protest at the head of the Shi'at Ali – or Party of Ali.

661
Ali murdered

680
Sunni majority defeat Shi'a in battle

1744
al-Wahhab's pact with House of Saud

Ismaili Muslims

The Ismaili Muslims are a Shi'a group, who today number around 17 million. The Nizari, by far the largest proportion of Ismailis, believe that their leader, the 49th Aga Khan, is a direct descendant of the Prophet. (Other Shi'a hold that the line has ended.) The Ismaili have their own unworldly spirituality based around searching for a hidden meaning in scripture, but they also managed to seize control of first Tunisia and then Egypt in the first half of the tenth century, and set up their own caliphate in Cairo that endured for 200 years. Whereas mainstream Shi'a Islam is literal, the Ismaili take a more mystical line. The Druze people of Lebanon and Syria are also associated with the Ismaili.

The final split The Battle of Karbala took place in 680 on the banks of the River Euphrates. It was a terrible defeat for the Prophet's direct descendants. Husain was starved into submission and butchered, along with many of his family, though two of his sons survived to take on the role of imam in the Shi'a movement. The Shi'a rejected the majority Sunnis (a term referring to their loyalty to the Sunnah, the Prophet's sayings and practices) as too worldly, preferring instead the religious purity of Ali and his family.

The Imam Husain Mosque at Karbala remains for the Shi'a – who make up 20 per cent of world Muslims – a holy site on a par with Mecca and a symbol of the martyrdom and injustice that pervades human life. Every year on the Day of Ashura, a memorial to the defeat of Husain, Shi'a men gather at the mosque to gash themselves with knives and beat their own backs with chains, recalling the brutality handed out by Yazid's troops.

> **Shi'ism was not brought into existence only by the question of the political succession to Muhammad, although this question was of course of great importance... [It] was not so much who should be the successor of Muhammad as what the function and qualifications of such a person would be.**

Hossein Nasr, 1979

A question of leadership

Those early battles defined the dividing lines in Islam that exist to this day. Who should lead the faithful? The most pious Muslim, as the Kharijites proposed? A direct descendant of the Prophet, as the Shi'a contended? Or an able administrator who strove for the peace and unity the Prophet so desired, as the Sunnis believed?

The Sunni/Shi'a wound has never healed. There are differences other than historical ones. The Shi'a have their own call to prayer (and can answer it three rather than five times). They venerate the tombs of their dead imams, including Ali's burial place at Najaf in Iraq, a practice that is considered heretical by the Wahhabis, part of the Sunni tradition.

Wahhabism

There were many revolts against the excesses of the Sunni ruling elites of the caliphate and later the Ottoman Empire. One prominent rebel was Muhammad ibn Abd al-Wahhab (1703–92), who led an anti-intellectual, anti-mystical and anti-establishment rising that promoted a return to the Qur'an and the Sunnah. Both, he said, were timeless and needed no updating or putting into context. He did not share Muhammad's tolerance towards other faiths, nor his progressive (for the seventh century) attitude to women, viewpoints that are demonstrated in his teaching, which became known as Wahhabism. By forming a pact in 1744 with the ruling house of Saud, al-Wahhab was able to shape an enclave of pure faith, which continues to this day in the form of Saudi Arabia, where Wahhabism is the dominant strand of Islam.

Other differences are more doctrinal. Shi'a lay greater emphasis on the Hadith, since it cements their link with the Prophet. Both Sunni and Shi'a believe that Allah has foreknowledge of all human action, but the Sunnis hold that he predestines it, something rejected by the Shi'a. Additionally, the mainstream of Shi'a Muslims, believing that the descendants of the Prophet have died out, give greater authority to living religious scholars – ayatollahs – to determine Islamic law and practice than do the Sunnis, who prefer to rely on past, and usually more moderate, wisdom.

the condensed idea
There are many approaches within Islam

29 The heart of Islam

The phrase 'the heart of Islam' refers to the Sufi mystical tradition. As Islam expanded into empire in the ninth and tenth centuries, it turned increasingly to jurists, who worked to distil the wisdom of the Qur'an, the Hadith and the Sunnah into the codes of Shar'iah law, a system that would give structure to society. Sufism was a reaction against this dry legalism, stressing love above justice. Its often uninhibited ceremonies, including songs and dancing, render it suspect in the eyes of many orthodox Muslims, but it remains a powerful force within the Islamic tradition.

The roots of Sufism are to be found in the eighth century, a time when the Islamic empire was growing in size, power and worldliness. Some Muslims recoiled at the luxury and wealth of the ruling elite that had come as a consequence of expansion. These dissidents, the Sufis, feared that their faith was becoming externalized into a 'state religion' and that in the process, Allah's message to the Prophet and to every individual Muslim was being corrupted.

The Sufis advocated a return to a simpler way of being, in which all Muslims were equal and differences were tolerated rather than proscribed by law. Followers of the Sufi ascetic path were distinguished by the coarse woollen garments they took to wearing; indeed, some people believe that their name comes from the Arabic word for wool, *suf*.

timeline

8th century	922
Sufism born	Husain al-Mansur executed

Women in the Sufi tradition

Sufism has traditionally afforded women greater freedom as leaders and intellectuals than elsewhere in Islam. Rabi'a al-Adawiyya (717–801) was one of a number of female teachers in early Sufism who insisted that Allah should be loved freely and willingly rather than because rules and laws frightened people into doing so. When she was a child, Muhammad had appeared in a dream to her father, identifying her as specially chosen, but famine hit her home city of Basra and she was sold as a slave. When her master heard her prayerful raptures, however, he freed her and told her that he was now her slave. She lived most of her life in the Iraqi desert, with no possessions, refusing all offers of marriage but attracting many disciples, to whom she taught the importance of truthfulness and self-criticism. She is sometimes credited as the founder of Sufi 'love-mysticism', which likens the state of spiritual ecstasy to falling in love with God.

Inner life The Sufi approach to faith is contemplative and monk-like, involving a withdrawal – practical and/or mental – from the concerns of the world, and stressing the need to abandon both ambition and self in order to uncover an inner spiritual life that will enable each believer to purify their heart and be one with Allah.

Sufis organize themselves into master and disciple units, or orders, with the master handing over the leadership to a chosen one amongst his followers on his death. Most masters claim a connection or blood link back to the Prophet Muhammad, often through his son-in-law Ali. One of the largest Sufi groups, the Naqshbandi, prefers instead to see itself as the successor of the first caliph, Abu Bakr.

> **Ascetism is not that you should not own anything, but that nothing should own you.**
>
> **Ali ibn Abi Talib,** *c.*11th century

> **You belong to the world of dimension, but you come from the world of non-dimension. Close the first shop and open the second.**
>
> Mevlana of Qonya, 1207–73

Sufis meet in *zawiyah*, places of learning and concentration, where they pray and meditate, using rhythmic breathing, fasting, vigils and chanting to heighten their awareness of God. Such rituals and practices soon attracted criticism from other Muslims. The use of music, poetry and dancing, often as a way of inducing spiritual uplift or even a trance-like state, was deemed to be un-Islamic. Talk of miracles and magic was attacked. When the Sufi master Husain al-Mansur claimed in 922 that a good Muslim could make the *hajj* in spirit while staying at home in body, he was executed for apostasy. Yet for all the suspicion they provoked, the Sufi have always remained part of mainstream Islam, and their approach and insights continue to be valued and appreciated.

Neo-Sufism

Neo-Sufism, another reform movement in Islam, grew up in the nineteenth century, thriving among North African Muslims in particular. Leaders such as Ahmad ibn Idris (1760–1836) in Morocco wanted to encourage people to be better Muslims but felt that traditional teaching was too legalistic and too divorced from everyday life in the region. Ibn Idris rejected the authority of every Muslim thinker since the Prophet, and urged his hearers to reflect and meditate on the life and example of Muhammad, rather than on past tradition, as the basis for deciding how to live ethically and justly in their own society. The Sanusiayyah movement, part of Neo-Sufism, remains the dominant form of Islam in Libya, while Neo-Sufi leaders such as Amir Abdul Kader in Algeria were prominent in anti-colonial resistance in the nineteenth century.

Spiritual context Abu Hamid al-Ghazzali (1058–1111), sometimes referred to as the Thomas Aquinas of Islam, was an expert in Islamic law. In 1095, he suffered a breakdown, which he later explained in terms of the realization that he knew much *about* God, but he did not know God himself. His solution was to embrace Sufi practice, which he distilled in 1105 into *The Revival of the Religious Sciences*, believed to be the most quoted Islamic book after the Qur'an and the Hadith.

Al-Ghazzali attempted to unite the external and internal life of Islam by giving Shar'iah law an ethical and spiritual context. Readers of his book were prescribed spiritual exercises, including *dhikr* (the chanting of divine names) to increase consciousness of God. Some Sufis, though, dismiss the idea that mystical insights can ever be committed to paper, maintaining that it would feel too much like externalizing them.

Golden age The period between the thirteenth and sixteenth centuries was the golden age of Sufism, a time when it became a genuinely popular movement. Many new orders were established. Jalal ud-Din Rumi, also known as the Mevlana of Qonya, founded one based on whirling dervishes (or seekers), teaching that gyration and music could lift the individual into the heavenly sphere. This was, he said, the purest form of Islam, or surrender to Allah.

In more recent times, however, the Sufi tradition has suffered repression. European colonizers who seized Muslim lands were particularly suspicious of the Sufis. Kemal Ataturk, the founder of modern Turkey in the twentieth century, was another who suppressed them – though not with enduring success. Most Sunni ruling elites today maintain close links with the Sufi orders, and the great Sufi shrines – in Baghdad, Ajmeer (India), Sylhet (Bangladesh) and Qonya (Turkey) – remain centres of pilgrimage.

the condensed idea
Islam has a mystical side

30 Militant Islam

In the twentieth century, many rulers of Muslim countries rejected what they saw as a medieval past by attempting to separate religion and politics. Ataturk in Turkey, Nasser in Egypt, Jinnah in Pakistan and the Shah in Iran were all encouraged by Western governments in their efforts to move with the times – insisting on modern dress, replacing Shar'iah with a civil legal system, and sidelining or exiling clerics. Such huge changes, however, inevitably provoked a backlash, and the later decades of the twentieth century and the opening one of the twenty-first have seen the rise of a new form of militant Islam.

During the nineteenth and twentieth centuries, the Western notions of secularism, nationalism, democracy and industrialization became pre-eminent. Societies that didn't adopt the model were regarded as backward, and in the push for markets and geopolitical dominance they were often swallowed up as colonies of European countries. Muslim states across northern Africa suffered this fate at the hands of France and Italy in the nineteenth century, and after the Ottoman Empire – 'the sick man of Europe' – had sided with defeated Germany in the First World War, its territories in the Middle East were divided as protectorates between Britain and France. A final symbol of the West's seizure of lands that Muslims had for centuries considered their own was the establishment in 1948 of the state of Israel on the territory of largely Muslim Palestine.

Religious and secular Some Muslim leaders reacted to the changing world by trying to adapt the Western model to their

timeline

1915	1948	1966
Fall of Ottoman Empire	Creation of state of Israel	Sayyid Qutb executed

countries. Others – notably the Ba'athists in Iraq and Syria – fused
socialism and Arab nationalism. All attempted in some measure to
impose a divide between the religious and the secular – and often
resorted to force when they were resisted. In Egypt in 1966, Sayyid
Qutb was executed by the secular nationalist leader, Gamal Abdel
Nasser (1918–70), whom he had branded an infidel. In Iran, the
Western-leaning government of Shah Muhammad Reza Pahlavi
(1944–79) exiled the Shi'a spiritual leader, Ayatollah Ruhollah
Khomeini (1902–89), only for the latter to inspire a revolution that
swept him to power.

Fatwa

Fatwas are Islamic legal opinions, issued by
jurists or spiritual leaders, clarifications of
the law when new circumstances or
questions arise for which the Qur'an and the
Sunnah offer no clear directive. The word
became internationally notorious in 1989
when Ayatollah Khomeini issued a *fatwa*
against the British novelist Salman Rushdie,
whom he judged to have produced a
blasphemous portrait of Muhammad in
his novel *The Satanic Verses*. Blasphemy
carries a death sentence. Khomeini's *fatwa*
was condemned by 48 out of 49 member
states of the Islamic Conference the month
after it was issued, but was only lifted nine
years later.

Khomeini had turned to history to characterize his struggle with the
Shah, likening it to the battle between Yazid and Husain at Karbala in
680 and claiming that the Shah was every bit as much an impostor as a
Muslim as Yazid had been. Islam could not be updated to suit economic
or political circumstances, he stressed. However, he then struggled with
modern militant Islam's first attempt to create a system of government
that satisfied his own view of history. The theocracy that is current-day
Iran uneasily combines Western democratic elections with a 'Supreme
Leader' drawn from the clerical elite.

1979	1994	2001
Fall of Shah of Iran	Taliban take control in Afghanistan	al-Qaeda destroy World Trade Center

Revisiting the past The new militant Islam was quick to annex other long-standing beliefs to its particular purposes. Abul Ala Mawdudi (1903–79), founder of the Jamaat-i-Islami party in Pakistan, and credited by many as a major influence on militant Islam, was among the first to invoke the Qur'anic notion of *jihad* – meaning, in its original form, simply 'struggle' – to promote a holy war against Western influences and those who attempted to introduce them. Meanwhile, Sayyid Qutb, a fundamentalist scholar, was fond of likening himself and his followers in Egypt to the original band who accompanied the Prophet when he was driven out of Mecca to Medina by corrupt city leaders.

Qutb's best known work, *Milestones*, published in 1964 and claiming Qur'anic blessing for violence and murder against 'infidels' (including all fellow Muslims who embrace secular values), is still much admired by extremist groups such as Islamic Jihad, Hizbollah in Lebanon and the dissident movement in Saudi Arabia. Though that country continues to be run according to a system inspired by puritan Wahhabist ideals from the eighteenth century, the spectacular riches it has acquired in recent times as a result of its oil reserves, as well as its ongoing alliance with the United States, has caused many there, including the founder of al-Qaeda, Osama bin Laden, to embrace militancy and murder.

Bin Laden planned his global campaign of terror from exile in Afghanistan, which from 1994 onwards was run by the militant Islamic Taliban government. Amongst its 'innovations' was to deny women

Yes, we are reactionaries, and you are enlightened intellectuals: You intellectuals do not want us to go back 1,400 years. You, who want freedom, freedom for everything, the freedom of parties, you who want all the freedoms, you intellectuals: freedom that will corrupt our youth, freedom that will pave the way for the oppressor, freedom that will drag our nation to the bottom.

Ayatollah Khomeini, 1979

Sayyid Qutb

The Egyptian teacher, novelist and poet Sayyid Qutb was, according to a university friend of the al-Qaeda leader Osama bin Laden, 'the one who most affected our generation'. Qutb divides Muslim opinion. To his admirers he was a martyr for the cause of true Islam. To his detractors he was a violent extremist. He welcomed Nasser's overthrow in 1952 of the pro-Western regime in Egypt, but soon grew disillusioned with the new ruler's secular nationalism. He was jailed in 1954 after an assassination attempt on Nasser and spent all but a few months of the rest of his life behind bars. He used the time to complete his still influential manifesto for political Islam, *Milestones*, and a 30-volume commentary on the Qur'an, where he advocated violent *jihad* and concluded that the Muslim world had no need of government, since individual Muslims simply had to follow the Qur'an and the Hadith. He was executed in 1966 on Nasser's orders.

education or work and to demand they cover every inch of their bodies when they went out in public. According to all mainstream Islamic scholars, such a policy went against the practice of the Prophet.

Suicide bombing In its efforts to react to a changing world dominated by the West, militant Islam preaches a return to traditional Muslim values, yet it has distorted and violated these, creating an impression in non-Muslim countries that the practices of the Taliban and al-Qaeda are described in the Qur'an and the Hadith. This is not the case. Suicide bombing, for instance, a favoured tactic of the extremist militant groups, has no basis in the Qur'an. Suicide is forbidden in Islam, while the killing of innocent bystanders is condemned as murder. 'Whoever kills the righteous along with the wicked,' wrote the Prophet, 'has nothing to do with me and I have nothing to do with him.'

the condensed idea
Militant Islam is in the minority

31 The many faces of Hinduism

Hinduism claims to be the oldest living religion in the world. It numbers one billion followers, of whom 90 per cent are in India. Modern Hinduism is the result of a complicated process of evolution and brings together many different strands. As a result, it is often described as more a way of life than a single religion. More accurately, it is a family of religions, a collection of cultural and philosophical systems that share neither a single founder, nor a commonly agreed sacred scripture, nor even a universal set of teachings.

The distant roots of what is now called Hinduism lie in the civilization that thrived in and around the Indus Valley – the 'Land of Seven Rivers', or Sapta-Sindhu (the origin of the word Hindu) – between 2500 and 2000 BCE. This ancient Indian empire was bigger in its time than either Egypt or Mesopotomia. When it was reinvigorated by Aryans from the steppes to the north, a series of sacred texts in Sanskrit began to emerge, known collectively as the Vedas ('knowledge'). There are four Vedas, which are acknowledged by all Hindus, of which the Rig Veda is the best known.

To begin with, those who followed this Vedic religion were travellers, traders and sometimes aggressors. From the seventh century BCE onwards, however, a group of mystics within the tradition began to advocate a change of heart to embrace peace and internal spirituality. Their

timeline

c.2500–2000 BCE	c.1500 BCE
Ancient civilization in Indus valley	Composition of Vedas

teachings are found in the Upanishads, which were strongly influenced by the Vedas and share their holy status in modern Hinduism.

It was from this Vedic religion of the Axial Age that Hinduism evolved, adding to what had hitherto been a severe and restrained tradition a dazzling array of colourful deities, effigies and temples. The name Hindu itself only started to be used around the thirteenth century CE, and Hinduism did not emerge as a defined religious entity until the eighteenth and nineteenth centuries, when India was learning to live with its European colonizers. This new Hinduism taught that because the divine was infinite, it could not be confined to a single expression – whether that be Brahman, the transcendent impersonal power beyond the universe, or Bhagavan or Ishvara, the Sanskrit words for 'Lord' and 'God', which designate a supreme creative and destructive power. Instead, a multitude of deities were worshipped, each expressing different aspects of the whole. Shiva and Vishnu are the most popular.

Brahma

There is a trinity (*trimurti*) of gods in Hinduism who between them cover life in this world. Alongside Vishnu and Shiva is Brahma (not to be confused with Brahman), whose role is the creation of the world and all its creatures (Hindus are mainly vegetarian out of respect for all created beings, with those who do eat meat avoiding cows). Brahma is depicted as having a red complexion, four heads – each reading one of the principal texts of the Vedas – four arms and a beard. Although described as the first of the three gods, and referred to alongside Vishnu and Shiva in all Hindu rites, he has very few temples devoted to him. There are many explanations for this in Hindu mythology, most of them variations on the tale that it is the result of a curse pronounced by Shiva on Brahma because he neglected his godly duties to pursue a woman, Shatarupa.

c.800–c.300 BCE
Emergence of 'Hinduism'

c.300 BCE
Bhagavad Gita

Vishnu and Shiva There are many schools in Hinduism, holding different philosophies and worshipping various forms of the divine. Put simply, these can be broken down into Vaishnavas, Shaivas, Shaktas and Smartas.

Vaishnavas – the largest group of the four – focus on Vishnu and his power to manifest himself in human form. On nine separate occasions, usually at times of great crisis, Vishnu has descended from heaven to save the Earth. Many believe that if he comes again, it will signify the end of the world. The best known of these manifestations have been as Krishna and Rama, both of whom are the subject of epic stories recalling how they acted heroically to restore the moral order and balance of the world. Vishnu is usually portrayed as having a human body, blue skin and four arms. He is commonly associated with light and sun.

Shaivas prefer Shiva, a contradictory character, sometimes ascetic, sometimes hedonistic, who destroys but only so as to recreate something more pure. Again Shiva is visualized in a human body, but with a third eye, for wisdom. Shaktas, meanwhile, look to the feminine, the Divine

Bhagavad Gita

The Bhagavad Gita ('The Song of the Lord') is one of the most influential texts in Hinduism, representing another link between the various branches of this family of religions. It was, most scholars concur, written during the late third century BCE and is ostensibly an accessible debate about the purpose of warfare. It consists of a dialogue between the warrior Arjuna and his friend Krishna, who reveals himself as the god Vishnu in human form. Arjuna is close to rejecting battle as futile, but Krishna persuades him that in certain circumstances it is necessary to fight in order to restore *dharma* to an otherwise destructive world. It is in outlining these circumstances that the Bhagavad Gita makes its impact, for it demands that everyone strive for detachment from and indifference to worldly gain. Moreover, it promises that this can be achieved not just by a favoured few but by all. 'If they rely on me,' Krishna tells Arjuna, 'even men born in the womb of evil reach the highest way.'

❝Those who, renouncing all actions in Me, and regarding Me as the Supreme, worship Me … For those whose thoughts have entered into Me, I am soon the deliverer from the ocean of death and transmigration … Keep your mind on Me alone, your intellect on Me. Thus you shall dwell in Me hereafter.❞

Bhagavad Gita, *c.***300** BCE

Mother, usually in the form of Lakshmi, a widely popular goddess, pictured as a beautiful woman with four arms who stands on a lotus flower. Her virtues are hard work, wealth, virtue and bravery. Finally, Smartas are devoted to five – or in some cases six – deities, who come together, they believe, to characterize the divine.

Indian nationalism The connection between Hinduism and Indian culture and national identity is an intimate one, and was encouraged by Indian nationalists in the nineteenth and twentieth centuries as they strove to cast off colonial rule. Other common threads that unite Hindus are the Vedas, certain ritual practices, and philosophical concepts such as *samsara* and *dharma*. *Samsara*, the cycle of birth, death and rebirth, governed by *karma*, is one of Hinduism's most important teachings, and is one that is also shared with other faiths.

Dharma refers in Hinduism to an overarching morality that guides how each individual treats others. It incorporates the imperative to be at the service of others, and of God, by acting virtuously and ethically. Each individual has their own *dharma*, known as their *sva-dharma*. The moral code of *dharma* is so central to Hinduism that an alternative name for the faith, often used by Hindus themselves, is Sanatana Dharma, Sanskrit for 'eternal law'.

the condensed idea
Hinduism is a family of religions

32 Hindu worship

Hindu patterns of *puja* or worship are numerous and diverse, and are woven into the social and cultural fabric of daily life in India. *Puja* can be undertaken as part of a crowd in a temple, but it is seen primarily as an individual pursuit and is just as valuable when done alone at home at a personal shrine or through meditating.

Hindu rites and rituals are deliberately designed to remind believers at every turn of the ubiquity of the divine. Their ultimate goal is *moksha* – or liberation from the cycle of birth, death and rebirth of *samsara* – which prefaces final union with Brahman in the afterlife.

There is no obligation for Hindus ever to go to temples. Many will only attend on great religious festivals. The principal focus of their devotion is the icons of the gods they keep in their homes. These icons are seen not just as images, but as manifestations of the divine (though in the pluralism that is Hinduism, some sects, such as the Arya Samaj, reject this notion). Prayer often takes the form of chanting or reciting from sacred scriptures.

Samskars *Samskars* – or sacraments – are rituals, many of them involving purification, that accompany all stages of life's journey. Mothers-to-be will undertake a ceremony to mark Punsavara (foetus protection) in the third month of pregnancy, Simantonnyaria in month seven to pray that the infant is healthy mentally as well as physically, and Jalakarma at childbirth, when honey is placed in the baby's mouth and the name of God is whispered in its ear (similar to the ritual in

> It is wonderful, the power of a faith [Hinduism] like that, that can make multitudes upon multitudes of the old and weak and the young and frail enter without hesitation or complaint upon such incredible journeys and endure the resultant miseries without repining. It is done in love, or it is done in fear; I do not know which it is. No matter what the impulse is, the act born of it is beyond imagination, marvelous to our kind of people, the cold whites.

Mark Twain, on Hinduism, 1895

Islam). Upanayana ('the sacred thread') is a ceremony held when a child starts at school.

Marriage is an elaborate and formal ritual with many well-established stages, starting from the moment the parents of the bride welcome the bridegroom to the wedding feast by placing a red dot – or *kumkum* – on his forehead. *Dharma* places great emphasis on compatibility between the bridal couple. Traditionally in India it has been thought that this is best achieved by parents arranging marriages for their children. Divorce is possible, but rates are extremely low.

Women in Hinduism The various schools of Hinduism disagree on the position of women. Viewpoints often depend as much on the social, cultural and economic backgrounds of believers as they do on the sacred texts, which are very muddled on the subject. In one Vedic marriage hymn, for example, it is stated that a wife 'should address the assembly as a commander'. Yet in 1987, the Indian government was still legislating to outlaw the ancient practice of *sati* – or *suttee* – in which a widow throws herself on her husband's funeral pyre. Some scriptures praise women who make this sacrifice. In traditional Hindu groups, widows are still required to wear distinctive white sarees, shave their heads, and remain largely hidden from public view, having handed over all their husband's worldly goods to their children. Some have to resort to begging to support themselves.

caste system

With religion and social practice so intertwined, the persistence of the caste system in India is often ascribed to Hinduism. This method of categorizing people traces its origins back to religious views about purity and the natural, god-given hierarchy. Caste was a word first used by Portuguese settlers. Hindus know the system better as the four *varnas*, in descending order: the Brahmins, or priests, believed to have emerged from Brahma's mouth; the Kshatriyas, or ruling/warrior class, who were made from Brahma's arms; the Vaishyas, merchants or artisans, who came from Brahma's thighs; and the Shudras, unskilled labourers and servants, who emerged from Brahma's feet. A fifth category of 'Untouchables' was added, those who were too lowly even to be part of the system. On to this basic categorization was imposed a more complex set of *jatis*, or layers, defined by birth, marriage and occupation. Caste still shapes Indian society, especially in rural areas, where marriage between *jatis*, though legal, is frowned upon. 'Untouchability', however, has been abolished by law.

Yoga The life of every Hindu is divided into four stages, known as *ashramas*: (1) Brahmacharya, the student stage, spent acquiring spiritual knowledge in celibate, controlled contemplation under the guidance of a guru; (2) Grihastha, the householder stage, involving marriage, parenthood and the establishment of a home; (3) Vanaprastha, the retirement stage, relinquishing material concerns and devoting more time to prayer and meditation; and (4) Sannyasa, preparing for and embracing death.

In navigating these four stages, there are thought to be several paths, or yogas. In the West, the word is associated with physical exercises, but in Hinduism it covers a whole array of physical, mental and spiritual

Pilgrimage

Hindus are encouraged to make pilgrimages – particularly in the third or Vanaprastha stage of their lives – as a way of achieving *moksha*. As well as various holy cities and temples, some of them gathered on a circuit for pilgrims, there is also the Kumbh Mela ('pitcher festival'), which takes place every four years, with the location alternating between Allahabad, Haridwar, Nashik and Ujjain, all of them on the banks of sacred rivers. The origins of the festival can be traced back to Vedic texts, in which the gods would regain their strength by churning an ocean of milk. Pilgrims who attend the festival take part in ritual bathing. As many as 70 million have been known to travel to the Kumbh Mela in a single year.

disciplines as described in various sacred texts. As many as 18 different yogas have been laid out, but the main four are: *bhakti* yoga – the path of love and devotion; *karma* yoga – the path of right action; *raja* yoga – the path of meditation; and *jnana* yoga – the path of wisdom and knowledge. All overlap, and none needs to be undertaken to the exclusion of others.

Festivals The main Hindu holy day is Diwali, the Festival of Lights, celebrated in late October or early November, depending on the advent of the new moon. As colourful as all Hindu ceremonies, it features fireworks, street celebrations and the lighting in every home of *diyas*, small clay pots filled with mustard oil into which are placed wicks of cotton string. These are said to guide the goddess Lakshmi into homes to bestow her blessings. Inspired by her presence, some Hindus choose this time of year to start new businesses. Others take advantage of another time-honoured religious tradition, which permits gambling at Diwali.

the condensed idea
Religion and culture mix in Hindu worship

33 Samsara

The cycle of birth, death and rebirth, known in Hinduism as *samsara* and elsewhere as reincarnation, stands in marked contrast to the ideas of the monotheistic religions about the finality of death and the nature of afterlife. Hinduism teaches of an ongoing and progressive judgement, sometimes over many lifetimes, dictated by *karma*, which roughly translates as the individual's actions in each lifetime, but which also includes the notion of an inheritance carried forward from one life to the next.

Karma is a Sanskrit word whose literal meaning is 'action'. It dates back to the Upanishads – and particularly to that written by Yajnavalkya, the personal philosopher of King Janaka of Videha, a leading supporter of the peaceful, internal spirituality that was reshaping Vedic beliefs from 800 BCE onwards.

Hitherto death had been seen as the preface to residence in the land of the gods for those who had correctly followed the rituals. Yajnavalkya and other Upanishadic sages proposed a new idea – that it was actions that counted, and that only when actions showed that a believer had freed himself from desire for all earthly things would he be liberated from the burden of sickness, old age and mortality in life after life, with no hope of final deliverance.

timeline
*c.*800 BCE
Upanishads define *karma* and *samsara*

That cycle of suffering was called *samsara*. It could only be broken by perfect self-knowledge, which would then lead to *moksha*, the ultimate liberation into everlasting union with the supreme God in an ill-defined heaven. These new ideas of *karma* and *samsara* were at first controversial, but by the fifth century BCE they had captured the mainstream of Hinduism.

Yajnavalkya

The sage and astronomer Yajnavalkya, who is credited as the author of, among other sacred texts, the Brhadaranyaka Upanishad, is a legendary and revered figure among Hindus. As a young student he is said to have angered his guru by taking too much pride in his own intellect. He was ordered to vomit up his knowledge as food, which was then consumed by his fellow students, who took the form of partridges. He had two wives. One of them, Maitreyi, asked him if she could achieve immortality by acquiring great wealth. He rebuked her, explaining that what she needed to do was seek throughout her life to understand the 'absolute self'. Only then would she find the path to infinite knowledge and therefore immortality. Yajnavalkya warned against trying to define the concept of *atman* – usually taken to mean 'soul' or 'self'. 'About this *atman*, one can only say "not, not" … He is ungraspable, for he cannot be grasped. He is undecaying for he is not subject to decay. He has nothing sticking to him, for he does not stick to anything. He is not bound; yet he neither trembles in fear nor suffers injury.'

c.500 BCE

New definitions widely accepted

Cause and effect *Karma* illustrates Hinduism's essential concern with how life is lived, as opposed to abstract principles of what is right and wrong. Hindus believe that every action, good or bad, has a consequence, either immediately, or during some life in the future. So bad deeds against *dharma* – known to Hindus as *paap* – bring bad *karma*, while good deeds (*punya*) result in good *karma*. However, there is more to this process than a simple cause and effect, with every individual responsible for their own destiny. Hindus also believe that the gods can intervene directly to change someone's *karma*.

A story is told – Hinduism is as fond of such stories as Christianity is of parables – about Sandipani, a guru of Krishna, the manifestation on earth of the god Vishnu. Sandipani has lost his son to a sea demon, who has taken him to Yama, the domain of the lord of death. This is said to be the result of the son's bad *karma*. Out of regard for his former teacher,

Prayopavesa

Prayopavesa, or fasting to death, is an accepted custom in Hinduism, but should not be equated directly with suicide. Strict conditions are applied. It must be done in a non-violent way and use natural means. It can be resorted to only when the body is exhausted and no longer functions. It cannot be undertaken impulsively: there has to be a time of preparation and for explaining to friends and relatives what is to happen. It must be entered into serenely, not when in a heightened

emotional state. In November 2001, Satguru Sivaya Subramuniyaswami, a noted leader of the Hindu community in the United States, took his own life by *prayopavesa*. He had terminal intestinal cancer. After spending a period in meditation, he refused all food and drank only water. He died after 32 days.

> **❛Our destiny was shaped long before the body came into being.❜**
>
> **Tulsidas, Hindu scribe, 1532–1623**

Krishna/Vishnu uses his authority to bring the son back from Yama and restore him to his father. He turns bad *karma* into good. It is precisely this power of influence – over and above the individual's own efforts – that for some Hindus proves the existence of God.

Varieties of *karma* There are several different sorts of *karma* in Hinduism. *Sanchita karma* is the total of *karma* from all past lives – a kind of accumulated debt. The portion of debt that the individual is working on in their current life is called the *Prarabdha karma*, while the *Agami karma* is what is to be added to or subtracted from the accumulated debt of each soul (*atman*) at the end of the present life. More fleeting is *Kriyamana karma* – sometimes called 'instant *karma*' – which is the *karma* created by trivial incidents in everyday life and which has no lasting effect.

There is debate among Hindus as to how *karma* operates within different groups. Some argue that children and animals cannot be held responsible for their actions and so are exempt from *Agami karma*. However, they do carry *Sanchita karma*. For all Hindus the key to liberation from *samsara* is to exhaust your *Sanchita karma*, something that can only be achieved by living an ethical life with the help of the gods.

the condensed idea
We all live many times

34 Jainism

For the past 2,600 years the Jains have shared with Hindus both the Indian subcontinent and many beliefs. However, this ancient, peace-loving religion, which has around four million followers, is distinct in several regards: its overarching concern for the universe; its belief in the spiritual equality of humans, animals and plants; and its extreme asceticism. Jains are all vegetarians; they shun worldly goods, sex and violence, and follow a path laid out in the sixth century BCE by an Indian prince-hermit named Mahavira.

Jains do not believe in God or gods, though they do hold that there are *jinas*, or pure souls, and *tirthankaras*, inspired teachers. Some would argue that they are atheists. They do, however, believe in the immortal soul. Their monk-like spiritual practices are based on a profound concern for the welfare of every living being in the universe – human, animal and plant – and for the health of the universe itself. They share with Hindus and Buddhists a belief in the cycle of *samsara*, but interpret it solely in terms of self-help. There are no gods to lend a helping hand.

Three rights Every Jain is responsible for his own efforts in adhering to the supreme principle of his faith, which is non-violence, and to the three 'jewels': right belief, right knowledge, and right conduct. In order to live according to these principles, Jains take five specific vows – or *mahavratas*. These are commitments to: non-violence; eschewing possessions; always telling the truth; never stealing; and sexual restraint.

Celibacy is regarded as the ideal state. The vows of the many Jain celibate monks and nuns are placed on a higher level than those of lay people who do marry and have children but who are committed to lifelong fidelity to their partner and an avoidance of sex for pleasure.

Jains believe that the first four of their vows were laid down by Parshva, the twenty-third *tirthankara* of their faith in this age. There have been other ages and many other *tirthankaras*, some of them women. There is some historical evidence that Parshva existed in the ninth century BCE and was of royal blood. The fifth vow was included at the behest of Mahavira – literally 'great hero' – who according to the Jain tradition lived between 599 and 527 BCE.

Following the death of his parents King Siddhartha and Queen Trishala, Mahavira (then Prince Vardhamana) abandoned the royal palace at the age of 30 and lived for the next 12 and a half years without possessions in search of enlightenment. When he finally found it, he spent the rest of his life teaching others how to attain it, collecting his wisdom in the sacred book known as the *Agamas*. On his death, Mahavira had achieved *moksha* – another concept shared with Hindus.

Fasting

Fasting plays a more prominent role in Jain spirituality than in other faiths and is undertaken more by women than men. Fasting purifies the body and the mind, in line with Mahavira's example and his emphasis on renunciation and asceticism. He is said to have abstained from food for six months at a time – a practice monks emulate to this day. Some take it a step further and fast for a whole year. It is not enough for a Jain simply not to eat. They must also stop wanting to eat. If they continue to desire food, the fast is regarded as pointless.

527 BCE
Death of Mahavira

350 BCE
Famine kills many Jain monks

19th century CE
Low point in Jain numbers

> **I bow down to those who have reached omniscience in the flesh and teach the road to everlasting life in the liberated state. I bow down to those who have attained perfect knowledge and liberated their souls of all karma. I bow down to those who have experienced self-realisation of their souls through self-control and self-sacrifice. I bow down to those who understand the true nature of soul and teach the importance of the spiritual over the material. I bow down to those who strictly follow the five great vows of conduct and inspire us to live a virtuous life.**
>
> **Namaskara Sutra: daily Jain prayer**

With their concern for the universe, Jains have a more developed map of the afterlife than Hindus, and describe a series of layers. In the centre is the 'Middle World', where humans must strive for enlightenment. Above it are two layers – one where liberated beings such as Mahavira live in perpetuity in a world without beginning (hence no creator god) or end, and one that is more of a staging post on the eternal journey to final enlightenment. Below it are two more layers – a series of seven hells, where beings are tormented by demons and by each other but from which they can escape, and finally a basement that holds the lowest forms of life for ever.

Jain influence Jainism has historically struggled in the shadow of Hinduism. When Hinduism is strong – for instance in the nineteenth century, as part of the resistance to colonization – Jainism has been weakened. Two distinct strands of the faith exist today – the Digambara Jains and the Svetambara Jains. The first are more austere. Their monks never wear clothes. They also take a more traditionalist line on, for example, the role of women, who, they say, can only reach final enlightenment after they have been reborn as men.

There is a powerful literary culture in Jainism. Jains founded some of India's oldest libraries. They are also found in disproportionate numbers

Jain vegetarianism

Jains are vegetarians, but because of their abhorrence of violence towards all living things (including plants), they do not consume root vegetables such as potatoes, garlic, onions, carrots and turnips. They will, however, eat rootstocks – turmeric, ginger and peanuts, for example. Aubergines are avoided because of the large number of seeds in them: a seed is seen as a carrier of budding life. Strict Jains do not eat food that has been left overnight, such as yogurt, and have their meals before sunset. The narrow practices of the Jain kitchen are found most markedly in Gujarati cuisine.

among the country's wealthy elite. Though they constitute only 0.2 per cent of the population, they pay more than 20 per cent of the tax revenue. Among those influenced by Jain ideas of non-violence was the independence leader Mahatma Gandhi.

The point of worship Jains insist that Mahavira was not the founder of their religion, but the last day on which he taught is recorded each year in the Jain version of the Hindu feast of Diwali. The other great feast, on which Jains attend their temples, is Paryushana, the birth of Mahavira; this is the culmination of eight days of fasting, repentance and rituals.

Since they do not have gods, and reject the notion of Mahavira being their founder, it may be asked why Jains worship at all. It is partly because of the influence of the wider Hindu culture in which they operate – though Jain rituals tend to be more restrained and austere. What the Jains do worship is the ideal of perfection achieved by Mahavira, Parshva and all other *tirthankaras* (none of whom can be verified historically). All who participate aspire to become pure souls.

the condensed idea
The world gets in the way of enlightenment

35 Sikhism

Sikhism was founded at the end of the fifteenth century by Guru Nanak, a Hindu who had studied Islam. The 20 million Sikhs (from the Sanskrit word for 'learner' or 'disciple') in the world today argue, however, that the body of beliefs he bequeathed is much more than simply a synthesis of Hinduism and Islam. It is his own distinctive creation, reinforced by the nine gurus who followed him, and subsequently by the Guru Granth Sahib, the Sikh holy book, which is today accorded the status of a living guru.

The charge that Sikhism is just a Hindu sect has been made repeatedly in India in recent decades, a reaction in part by Hindu nationalists to the conflict between the Indian state and the large number of Sikhs in Punjab. In June 1984, Indian troops stormed the Sikhs' holiest shrine, the Golden Temple at Amritsar. Four months later, the Indian Prime Minister, Indira Gandhi, was assassinated by two of her bodyguards, both Sikhs. Her death unleashed bloody intercommunal violence that left an estimated 10,000 people dead, though some sources say it was as many as 17,000.

A religion of service There are plenty of beliefs shared by Hinduism and Sikhism – notably *samsara*, the cycle of birth, death and rebirth – and Islam and Sikhism are both monotheist religions. Yet Sikhism has its own unique character, based on its overriding duty of service – to God and to the community. It differs therefore from

timeline

1469	1699
Birth of Guru Nanak	Guru Gobind Singh declares Khalsa

Hinduism in the weight it gives to the subjugation of the individual to society.

If ethical questions arise that have no ready answer in the Guru Granth Sahib or in the Gurmat (the collective wisdom of the gurus), Sikhism teaches that they should be resolved by the whole community of the faithful, or Khalsa. Actions are held to be more important than rituals, and followers are encouraged to put aside their *haumain* – self-centred pride, which attaches them to things of this world – and instead search inside themselves for enlightenment.

The Five Ks Sikhs have a distinctive appearance, dating back to the time of the ninth and final guru to follow Guru Nanak. In 1699, Guru Gobind Singh decreed what are called by Sikhs the 'Five Ks'. He intended them as a means of identifying the Khalsa and creating a bond between them. They are: Kesh (uncut hair); Kara (a steel bracelet); Kanga (a wooden comb); Kaccha (cotton underwear); and Kirpan (a steel sword). Male Sikhs also wear turbans.

Sikh rituals

When a baby is born, Sikhs whisper the words of the Mool Mantar (a prayer composed by Guru Nanak) into its ear and place honey in its mouth. Within 40 days the child will be taken to the gurdwara (temple) for a baptism ceremony using holy water. The Sikh marriage ceremony, based on the guidance of the gurus, is called Anand Karaj, and is open only to couples who are both Sikhs. Though conscious of Guru Nanak's teaching that ritual plays a secondary role, Sikhs are keen on processions, though they eschew icons. They mark Diwali, but as a commemoration of the release from prison in 1619 of the sixth guru, Hargobind Singh. Their largest festival, however, is Vaisakhi, to mark the New Year and the birth of the Sikh people as Khalsa in 1699.

1799	1919	1984
Independent Sikh state established	Amritsar massacre by British	Storming of Golden Temple by Indian troops

> **'Realization of truth is higher than all else.
> Higher still is truthful living.'**

Guru Nanak, 1469–1539

Each of the Five Ks has its own symbolism. Hair is regarded by Sikhs as a sign of both holiness and strength. To leave it uncut indicates that they are willing to accept God's gift to them as it was intended. The origins of the Kachha and the Kirpan lie in the often violent history of Sikhism, which has been forced to assert itself to maintain its distinct identity in the shadow of the larger Hindu and Muslim groups that surround its homeland on the India–Pakistan border. The Kachha was the favoured dress of Sikh warriors in the eighteenth century, while the Kirpan recalls the 'soldier-saints' summoned by Guru Gobind Singh to defend Sikhism.

Guru Nanak Guru Nanak set out the basis of Sikhism in a series of highly poetic writings, which form the basis of Sikh scripture. Historians have found little actual evidence of his life, but his followers have woven a rich garment of stories around him. One tells how, at the age of 11, he refused to wear the 'sacred thread', a custom for Hindu boys of his age and caste in his native Punjab. People should be distinguished by the things they did, he insisted, rather than by what they wore.

Guru Nanak's principal argument with Hinduism and Islam was that both placed too much emphasis on the externals – pilgrimages, penances and poverty – and too little on the internal changes necessary in each believer's soul. He taught that there was only one God, who was without form or gender, and who treated all as equal regardless of whether they were male or female, high caste or 'Untouchable'. He also maintained that there was no need to go through priests or rituals to have a relationship with God.

Fight for survival It was under the fifth of Guru Nanak's successors, Guru Arjan Dev (1563–1606), that the Sikhs began their long fight for survival. The Mughal emperor Janaghir (ruled 1605–27)

Duties and vices

Sikhs believe that liberation from *samsara* is possible only by the grace of God. In this context they specify three duties involved in serving God and five vices that separate believers from him. The duties are: Nam Japna – keeping God in mind at all times; Kirt Karna – earning an honest living; and Vand Chhakna – giving to charity and caring for others. The five vices are: lust; covetousness; attachment to things of this world; anger; and pride.

was alarmed by Guru Arjan's success in expanding the Sikh capital, Amritsar, and was determined to bring the Sikhs to heel. In 1606 he had the guru executed, but the battle continued under Arjan's successor, with the Mughals trying to force the Sikhs to convert to Islam.

It was Guru Gobind Singh (1666–1708) who finally refashioned the Sikhs into both a community and a military force capable of defending itself. A poet, philosopher and warrior, he succeeded his father as guru at the age of nine. In 1699 he declared all Sikhs part of Khalsa, set out guidelines on how they should dress, and summoned the soldier-saints. When he died, he ordered that there should be no more human gurus, but only the holy book.

The military leaders who followed Guru Gobind succeeded by the end of the eighteenth century in setting up an independent Sikh state in the Punjab, even though Sikhs were in a minority there. Initially opposed to British rule in India, they became close allies of the Raj until a massacre of Sikhs in 1919 at Amritsar soured relationships. When the Punjab was partitioned in 1947 between newly created India and Pakistan, the Sikhs felt they had been ignored, a grievance that led directly to the violence of the 1980s.

the condensed idea
Serve others to serve God

36 Buddha and the Bodhi tree

Buddhism is distinct from most other religions in that it does not hold with the idea of a personal God. Instead, it concentrates on individual spiritual development and the search for enlightenment, based on the teachings and experience of Siddhartha Gautama, a sixth-century BCE royal prince turned wandering monk who confronted head on the question of human suffering.

Siddhartha Gautama abandoned his wife, his newborn child and his parents – who wept as he swapped his fine clothes for a monk's simple yellow robe and cut his hair off with a sword – to spend six years roaming northern India, struggling to reconcile the pain that he saw in the world around him with the Vedic religion of India. He lived as an ascetic, rejecting all comforts and luxuries, and was disciplined in his life of prayer and meditation, but all to no avail. A part of him – what he termed his 'shadow self' – remained rooted in this world and held him back from enlightenment.

In his despair, he relaxed his regime and sat for three days and three nights under a large fig tree. At his lowest point, Gautama finally laid to rest that shadow self and understood *dharma* – the same word used by Hindus but which he described as the law (or truth) that reflects the fundamental principles of existence. Ignorance of the true nature of humankind, he perceived, was the real cause of suffering in the world.

timeline

563 BCE	**528 BCE**
Siddhartha Gautama born	Moment of enlightenment

> **Thousands of candles can be lighted from a single candle, and the life of the candle will not be shortened. Happiness never decreases by being shared.**

The Buddha, 6th century BCE

With this realization he achieved spiritual enlightenment and saw the world with new eyes. The tree is called the Bodhi tree, or tree of enlightenment, and Gautama became the Buddha, 'the enlightened one'. He spent his remaining years on Earth trying to help others to reach the same state of awareness, insisting that it was a path all could follow.

Buddhist scriptures The story of Buddha is contained in the Buddhist scriptures, a many-volumed collection of a variety of origins. At first the account was passed on in the oral tradition by Buddha's original disciples, a community of monks – the *sangha*. It was only around the third century BCE that the story was written down. There has always been much dispute, though rarely conflict, over the authenticity of the various texts. The version preferred by many scholars

The Mahabodhi Temple

The spot where Buddha made his spiritual breakthrough is today the site of the Mahabodhi – or 'great awakening' – Temple. It is 60 miles from Patna in Bihar state in eastern India and is a UNESCO World Heritage Site. In 250 BCE, a Buddhist monastery was established there by the Emperor Asoko. The current building – which features four smaller towers around a central one that is 180 feet tall – was completed in the fifth century CE. Buddhists believe this place to be the 'navel of the world', and that it will be the last placed destroyed at the end of time.

483 BCE	**3rd century BCE**	**250 BCE**
Buddha dies	Buddhist scriptures written down	Mahabodhi Temple built

is that from the first century BCE in the Pali dialect of northern India – a close relative of the tongue Buddha himself would have spoken.

What makes the Buddhist scriptures unusual is that they tell us very little about the life of Buddha. They are not a biography and they deliberately shun the idea of focusing on his personality. The details of his life that emerge do so as anecdotes he drops into sermons.

There are three essential strands or baskets (*tipitaka*) in the Buddhist scriptures: the discourses or sermons; the disciplines, a set of rules and practices for those who wish to follow Buddha by joining his monastic order; and a disparate collection of more philosophical material.

Four noble truths The essence of Buddha's teaching was contained in a discourse he delivered in the deer park at Samath to his first students. It is known as 'the Discourse on the Four Noble Truths'. These truths are: Dukkha, the truth of suffering; Samudaya, the truth of the origin of suffering; Nirodha, the truth of the cessation of suffering; and Magga, the truth of the path to the cessation of suffering. Sometimes

The early life of Siddhartha Gautama

Although the Buddhist scriptures tell us little about Buddha's early life, tradition teaches that he was born around 563 BCE in the small kingdom of Kapilvastu in what is today Nepal. His father was King Suddhodana and his mother Queen Maha Maya. Some accounts say she died giving birth to him. Others recount how a hermit seer came to see the baby and predicted that he would be a holy man. As a young man, Gautama lived a life of luxury, with three palaces built for him. At 16 he married his cousin, Yasodhara, and had a son, Rahula. Some texts say that he turned his back on this life at the age of 29. His death is traditionally placed in 483 BCE, but scholars today suggest it was around 400 BCE.

Buddhists liken Buddha to a doctor. In the first two truths he saw, diagnosed and identified the cause of suffering. In the third he realized it could be cured. And in the fourth he prescribed that cure.

> **He who sees me sees the dharma and he who sees the dharma sees me.**
> The Buddha, 6ᵗʰ century BCE

Buddha blamed suffering on desire, *tanha*. Desire could, he conceded, be positive, but he identified three negative types – greed, ignorance and hatred – all of which lead to destructive urges. In one of his best-known discourses, the 'Fire Sermon', he described humankind as 'burning with the fire of lust, with the fire of hate, with the fire of delusion. I say it is burning with birth, ageing and death, with sorrows, with lamentations, with pains, with griefs, with despairs.'

To avoid such burning, he held out the third Noble Truth – the possibility of liberation to Nirvana, the state of reaching enlightenment, where the fire was put out and replaced with spiritual joy that was without fear or emotional excess.

Eightfold Path To attain *Nirvana*, Buddhists are urged to follow the Eightfold Path, part of the fourth Noble Truth. 'I saw an ancient path, an ancient road, travelled by the Rightly Self-awakened Ones of former times,' Buddha says in the scriptures. 'And what is that ancient path, that ancient road, travelled by the Rightly Self-awakened Ones of former times? Just this noble eightfold path: right view, right aspiration, right speech, right action, right livelihood, right effort, right mindfulness, right concentration … I followed that path.' What guided him above all was the practice of meditation, which lies at the heart of the Buddhist tradition.

the condensed idea
Humans must strive
for *dharma*

37 Schools of Buddhism

There are today an estimated 350 million Buddhists around the globe. They follow a variety of schools, all of them focused on the Buddha, but placing the emphasis on different aspects of his teaching. The original *sangha* or monastic community of Buddhists has evolved into a diverse body of faithful that encompasses both the traditional Theravada school, dominated by monks, and the broader Mahayana school, which spread out across Asia.

The differences of opinion about how precisely to follow Buddha's teachings started to appear at a great council held about 100 years after his death. The Theravada, 'the school of the elders', retains at its core the monkish *sangha* that dates back to Buddha's first disciples. It is strongest among the majority Sinhalese community in Sri Lanka and in south-east Asia.

Mahayana – 'the great vehicle' – is found more in east Asia and has a number of manifestations, including Pure Land, Zen and Tibetan Buddhism. It has its own stages or classifications – the three *yanas*, or vehicles. The largest one is the central, everyday Mahayana grouping. Then there is the more traditional Hinayana, often called 'the narrow way', with stress placed on meditation, simple living and personal and spiritual discipline. Finally there is the Vajrayana, which literally means 'diamond' or 'indestructible vehicle', and has been especially influential

timeline

5th century CE	7th century CE
Bodhidharma takes Buddhism to China	Hui Neng teaches Zen Buddhism

in Tibet. It tends to be the most colourful of the three, and includes the Tantric tradition.

Mahayana Buddhists have a metaphor to describe the relationship between the three *yanas*. The Hinayana is the foundation of the palace of enlightenment. The Mahayana provides its walls and superstructure. The Vajrayana is its golden roof. All are essential for the building to function but one may be more eye-catching than the others.

Buddha principle There is one essential contrast between Theravada and Mahayana Buddhism, and this arises over the question of Buddha's humanity. Theravada teaches that Buddha was a wise human being who demonstrated how to achieve Nirvana. His example is all that Buddhists need. Mahayana Buddhists distinguish between the historical Buddha and what might be called a 'Buddha principle', an eternal presence that is open to all and indeed part of all. This is akin to the status of Brahman in Vedic/Hindu thought, which much influenced Buddhism as it evolved, and allows for more than human effort alone in escaping the cycle of *samsara* and achieving Nirvana.

Bodhidharma

There are few facts and much legend surrounding Bodhidharma. He is said to have been born of royal stock in the southern Indian state of Kerala, but to have rejected his background and travelled as a Buddhist monk across Malaysia, Thailand and Vietnam before arriving in China. He was also an expert in martial arts. His relationship with Emperor Wu of the Liang dynasty was never an easy one, but he did manage to secure a place for Buddhism on Chinese soil. Bodhidharma taught the technique of wall-gazing – looking at a wall or blank object to focus the mind in meditation. He is said to have spent nine years in a single stretch looking at a wall. Buddhists count him as the twenty-eighth patriarch in a direct line back to Buddha, and as the first patriarch of the Zen (or Chan) school of Buddhism in China.

8th century CE	**9th century CE**	**13th century CE**
Padmasambhava goes to Tibet	Buddhism under strain in India	Buddhism dies out in India

Spread of Buddhism In the third century BCE, under the patronage of the Emperor Ashoka, Buddhism spread and flourished throughout India as a religion of the many, rather than of the elite as previously. For many centuries it co-existed with Hinduism and Jainism, but from the ninth century CE onwards it declined in the face of a popular revival of Hinduism, which blurred the lines between the two faiths. It came under further pressure in the eleventh century from aggressive Muslim rulers, and by the thirteenth century had all but vanished from its motherland. Its schools, however, continued to thrive elsewhere in Asia.

Buddhism had started to filter along the Silk Road trading route from the first century CE. It is a fifth-century Indian Buddhist monk called Bodhidharma who is credited with firmly establishing it in China, where it mixed with the local religion, Taoism, and flowered, developing its own Mahayana schools, notably Pure Land and Zen. The latter arose in the seventh century CE, when the revered teacher Hui-Neng gave Buddhism a distinctively Chinese character.

Zen practice Zen is built on two practices – meditation and study. It emphasizes that enlightenment is to be found above all in the present moment, and rejects – with a vehemence unmatched elsewhere in Buddhism – ritual and intellect in favour of an instinctive spiritual enlightenment that is directly transmitted from master to student.

"When alive, one keeps sitting without lying down.
When dead, one lies without sitting up.
In both cases, a set of stinking bones!
What has it do with the great lesson of life?
With those who are sympathetic
Let us have discussion on Buddhism.
As for those whose point of view differs from ours
Let us treat them politely and thus make them happy.
(But) disputes are alien to our School,
For they are incompatible with its doctrine."

Hui-Neng, 7th century CE

> **Those who turn from delusion back to reality, who meditate on walls, the absence of self and other, the oneness of mortal and sage, and who remain unmoved even by scriptures are in complete and unspoken agreement with reason.**

Bodhidharma, 5th century CE

In Tibet, all attempts to replace the indigenous faith, Bon, were rebuffed until in the eighth century King Trisongdetsen invited an Indian master to the country. Padmasambhava, the 'Lotus-born', came from the Vajrayana school, which dates back to the first century CE. Also sometimes called the Tantra, it teaches that enlightenment can be accessed anywhere, in any walk of life. The essential thing is to adapt and follow the body's natural patterns, desires and energies in the search for spiritual awakening. So – in perhaps the most often reported of Tantric teachings – sex is seen as having a spiritual purpose if individuals devote enough time to practising it.

The Tibetan Book of the Dead

One of the best-known Buddhist texts in the Western world is the *Tibetan Book of the Dead*, more properly termed 'Liberation Through Hearing During the Intermediate State'. It is said to have been written by Padmasambhava, and covers a stage called *bardo*, which lasts from the onset of death through to rebirth in the next incarnation. The book includes meditations, prayers, mantras and guidance on the signs of death and rebirth. It describes six stages, including an intermediate period of seeing visions of Buddha.

the condensed idea
Buddhism blossomed in China

38 Buddhist wheel of life

Buddhists follow a number of daily practices in their various traditions, but there remains a core of shared concerns and aspirations, most notably liberation from the pain of *samsara* by achieving eternity in Nirvana. High on the list of trademark Buddhist rituals and disciplines are meditation and a series of colourful festivals, centred on the temple, that celebrate the wisdom of Buddha.

The most important of the shared Buddhist festivals is Wesak/Vesak/Vaisakha, marked each year in May and often referred to as Buddha's birthday. It recalls not only his birth but also his life and his enlightenment. On that day, Buddhists go to their temples, carrying flowers. There they pray, meditate and light candles and joss sticks. Some take part in a ceremony in which a statue of a baby Buddha is washed. Those who participate are purified of their own bad *karma*.

Other significant dates in the Buddhist calendar are Dharma Day, when believers give thanks for the wisdom of Buddha and all the enlightened teachers, or bodhisattvas, who have followed in his wake. Theravada Buddhists place particular emphasis on the festival of Kathina, which recalls Buddha's alms-giving. In Tibetan Buddhism, the great festival is Losar, or New Year, while in some traditions Parinirvana – also known as Nirvana Day – marks Buddha's death and is an occasion for reflecting on the cycle of life, death and rebirth.

timeline

Early February	Late February
Nirvana Day	Losar

Nirvana

Nirvana – or Nibbana in the original Pali dialect version of the Buddhist scriptures – is not a concept unique to Buddhism. The Buddha described it as 'the highest happiness'. It is not essentially a place but a state of being, free from craving, anger and greed and awash in peace and compassion. Those who attain Nirvana are freed from *samsara*, they have no new *karma* and they stay in this ideal state for eternity. Buddhism resists descriptions of Nirvana. Buddha said it was simply 'consciousness without feature, without end, luminous all around'.

Buddhist rituals can be performed alone, at home, or in a monastery or temple. All have equal status. However, the temples have both a communal and a symbolic role in Buddhism. Their design has to incorporate five elements – fire, air, earth, water and wisdom. Earth is usually represented by a square base and wisdom by a pinnacle at the top of the building.

Traditionally worship takes place sitting barefoot on the floor, facing an image of Buddha and chanting. There may also be monks chanting from the scriptures, and occasionally music. The mantra – a word or phrase repeated over and over again – is another feature of worship. It is believed to influence the individual's spiritual state and his capacity to focus on his inner life. Sometimes mantras are printed on flags decorating the temple. Buddhists also use prayer beads as they chant.

> **❝All that we are is the result of what we have thought: it is founded on our thoughts, it is made up of our thoughts.❞**
>
> **Dhammapada (Buddhist scripture)**

April	May	December
Theravada New Year	Wesak ('Buddha Day')	Bodhi Day

> **All living things fear being beaten with clubs.**
> **All living things fear being put to death.**
> **Putting oneself in the place of the other,**
> **Let no one kill nor cause another to kill.**

Dhammapada (Buddhist scripture)

Meditation Buddhists insist that meditation be undertaken with both body and mind, so as to avoid 'duality'. By meditating, they seek to turn away from the world, its activities and its concerns, and connect with an inner life of thoughts, feelings and perceptions. Meditation is regarded as the means of accessing key mental states such as calm, concentration and one-pointedness. This last state is made up of six distinct forces: hearing, pondering, mindfulness, awareness, effort and intimacy.

Posture is also important in meditating successfully in all forms of Buddhism, but in Zen it receives particular emphasis. A key Zen practice is Zazen. This involves sitting in one of several recommended positions to meditate. The classic position is the Lotus, in which the individual sits cross-legged with the left foot on top of the right thigh and the right foot on top of the left thigh.

Bhavachakra One of the most common images in Buddhism is the Bhavachakra, or wheel of life. This is a mandala, the sort of complex diagram with spiritual and ritual significance found originally in Hinduism but taken up by Buddhists, particularly in the Tibetan tradition, where it is made from coloured sand to highlight the transitory nature of life.

The Bhavachakra attempts to sum up the Buddhist vision of the universe and the cycle of birth, death and rebirth. It is usually divided into five or six realms. These are: the realm of the gods (itself then often subdivided into as many as 26 levels), where the gods live long lives in pleasant surroundings but still struggle towards final enlightenment and Nirvana; the realm of humans; the realm of the hungry ghosts, occupied by those who are preoccupied with worldly goods but who are also disappointed, and sometimes symbolized by figures with huge bellies but small mouths, craving food but unable to eat enough to be full; the realm of animals – which are not capable of enlightenment, but which should be treated with kindness; and finally the realm of hell, a place of torture but a transitory state.

The ethical life Buddhists are expected to take full personal responsibility for everything they do and for the consequences that follow from their actions. In living an ethical life, they take several distinctive stances. One of these is the belief that it is wrong to hurt or kill animals, because humans and animals are seen as very closely connected, not least by *samsara*, in which individuals may be reborn in the realm of animals.

Shaolin monks and Kung fu

The Shaolin order is a Buddhist sect founded in the fifth century CE and based at the Zen temple in Dengfeng in China. It is best known in the West for its role in developing the martial art of kung fu. The temple has had a chequered past, having been attacked, destroyed and rebuilt many times. It was this history of aggression against it that prompted the monks to learn kung fu so as to defend themselves. However, Shaolin teaching forbids any monk from ever being the aggressor, and enjoins them to use the minimum force necessary for self-defence.

Buddhists also preach and practise non-violence. 'Even if thieves carve you limb from limb with a double-handed saw,' warned Buddha, 'if you make your mind hostile you are not following my teaching.' Many Buddhists are therefore pacificists. Monks are permitted to defend themselves, but may not kill another, even in self-defence. Buddhist monks, however, have been pioneers in the martial arts. The Shaolin order of monks, famed for its fighting prowess, is perhaps the best known.

the condensed idea
Nirvana is a state of being

39 Confucianism

The Chinese philosopher Confucius (551–479 BCE) regarded himself as neither an original thinker nor the founder of a religion. He was, he said, a 'transmitter' of existing ideas, gathered by studying the wisdom of the past and applying it to the present. Confucius's ethical system – called Li – strove to define moral behaviour for rulers and the ruled alike, and was based above all on justice and sincerity. That system continues to exert a profound influence over the lives of billions of people in countries such as China, Korea and Vietnam, with some 350 million today describing themselves as Confucians.

Scholars warn that accounts of the life of Confucius should not be treated as fact. However, Records of the Grand Historian, the renowned chronicle of Chinese history, written four centuries after his death, tells that he was born in the city of Qufu in the state of Lu, now part of Shandong province in China. His name in Chinese is Kong Fuzi, but was rendered in English as Confucius.

Confucius came from what might, in modern terms, be called the middle classes. His father was an elderly noble whose marriage to a much younger woman had caused scandal and forced him out of his privileged place in society. Confucius had to work for a living, and was at various stages a clerk and a bookkeeper.

Five Classics Through study, ability and application, Confucius climbed his way up the ladder to be justice minister in Lu by the age of

timeline

551 BCE	532 BCE	498 BCE
Birth of Confucius	Confucius marries	Appointed justice minister in L

53. However, disillusioned with the moral laxity of his master, he resigned and journeyed for 15 years round north-east and central China, sharing his thoughts on good governance and living an ethical life. He spent the last four years of his life back home, teaching his disciples, who along with his grandson, Zisi, spread his ideas far and wide.

Confucius is believed by his admirers to have distilled his teaching into what are known as the Five Classics. They are: Classic of Changes (also known as the I Ching), Classic of Poetry, Classic of Rites, Classic of History and Spring and Autumn Annals. Though still venerated by Confucians, these books are now thought unlikely to be the work of Confucius himself, but rather the product of later generations of disciples eager to spread his wisdom.

The Analects The true classic text of Confucianism is the Analects, a collection of sayings and discourses by Confucius, compiled by his disciples from around 50 years after his death in an attempt to turn his teaching into a system of belief and practice. So successful did this prove that by 140 CE, under the Hang dynasty, which ruled a recently united China, Confucianism became the official imperial philosophy, remaining the bedrock of Chinese officialdom until the nineteenth century.

Confucius drew his ideas from a range of sources – including Indian sages and

Matteo Ricci

The Italian Jesuit priest Matteo Ricci (1552–1610) was the first European to be allowed to enter the bastion of the Chinese emperors, the Forbidden City in Beijing. He also produced the first translations of Confucius's writings into Latin, having already devised the first Chinese–Portuguese dictionary. Ricci had made his way to China via the Portuguese colony of Goa in India, and lived there from 1582 until his death, when the Emperor waived the rule requiring that foreigners be buried in the Portuguese enclave at Macao, and instead designed a Buddhist temple in Beijing for the purpose.

483 BCE Returns from his travels to teach

479 BCE Dies

c.430 BCE Analects compiled

> **With coarse rice to eat, with water to drink, and my crooked arm for a pillow – is not joy to be found therein? Riches and honours acquired through unrighteousness are to me as the floating clouds.**
>
> Confucius

Chinese traditional beliefs. He stands alongside Buddha as one of the key figures of the Axial Age (800–300 BCE), a time when understanding of religion was undergoing a profound shift around the world.

Personal perfection As a political philosophy, Confucianism advocates rule by the most able, not necessarily by the high-born. The distinction between the political and the social/ethical/moral, however, soon blurs, for Confucius, in promoting a hierarchical system of governance, also insisted that rulers (as well as the ruled) should aim for personal perfection. They must study, draw on the past, and use their judgement as to what is in the best interests of all. In short, they must set an example – precisely what Confucius himself did.

Confucius, then, is a role model, not a deity. His code is based on his own reactions, rather than on abstract theory about human behaviour. It should be stressed, however, that he was not a sceptic. He was devout in following traditional rituals of ancestor worship, and spent long periods in silence in what we would now call prayer. But his concerns were down-to-earth, not esoteric. Learn to serve men first, he told his disciples, then worry about the gods.

Here and now Confucius said nothing about the afterlife. There is no indication in his teaching of the sort of interest in matters of the spirit and the soul that distinguishes other religions. Instead he concerned himself with a vision that drew extensively on existing Chinese practices, such as ancestor worship, the primacy of the family (*hsiao*), respect for elders, and loyalty. This ethical approach, which he called Li, has three main pillars.

The first of these pillars is concerned with rites and rituals and is based on ceremonies associated with sacrifice to ancestors and ancient deities. Confucius believed that these were the cornerstone of individual ethical behaviour and of social cohesion. 'Respectfulness, without the rites, becomes laborious bustle,' he states in the Analects. 'Carefulness, without the rites, becomes timidity; boldness, without the rites, becomes insubordination; straightforwardness, without the rites, becomes rudeness.'

The second pillar is social and political institutions. Confucius was no revolutionary, but he did want the existing system to work better for the benefit of all. He preferred the idea of a single emperor ruling China rather than a series of smaller states forever at war. That emperor should, he suggested, display outstanding qualities of honesty and truthfulness. It was these attributes that would command the respect of his subjects. If the emperor failed to show them, he did not deserve to rule.

The final pillar concerns the etiquette of daily behaviour. Here Confucius promoted the concept of *yi* – righteousness, or what is ethically right – as the guiding light for individuals and societies. The opposite of self-interest, *yi* teaches that the greater good must always come before individual benefit.

Ren

Ren is a key principle in Confucius's ethical teaching. It is a word that doesn't translate easily into a single English equivalent but instead means something between benevolence, humaneness and selflessness. 'If the people be led by laws, and uniformity sought to be given them by punishments, they will try to avoid the punishment but have no sense of shame,' says Confucius in the Analects. 'If they be led by virtue, and uniformity sought to be given them by the rules of propriety, they will have the sense of shame and moreover will become good.'

> **We are allowed to hear our Master's views on culture and the cultural insignia of goodness, but about the ways of heaven, he will not tell us anything.**
>
> **Zigong, one of Confucius's first disciples**

the condensed idea
Put others first

40 Confucius and the Communists

When Confucius died, he bequeathed to his followers a body of philosophical thought. It was the achievement of successive generations of his disciples to fashion this into a religious system that was to became part of the social and political make-up of China. Such a partnership with secular authority has inevitably brought conflict and challenges, not least with the advent of the Communist People's Republic of China in 1949. During the 'Cultural Revolution' between the mid-1960s and mid-1970s, Confucianism was attacked and persecuted, but in more recent times it has regained its influence.

Confucius's family played a role in the development of his thoughts into a system. His grandson Zisi continued his philosophical school after his death, and even today, one of his direct descendants, Kong Tsui-chang, who lives in Taiwan, is venerated as the seventy-ninth in a line that leads straight back to Confucius. It was his disciples, however – notably Mencius (372–289 BCE) and Xun Zi (312–230 BCE) – who did most to ensure that Confucius left a lasting mark on Chinese civilization, by organizing his teachings into a religious and social force. By 221 BCE, when the King of Qin conquered the neighbouring states and declared himself Emperor Shi Huang Di of China, Confucianism was already a powerful movement. So much so, in fact, that Huang Di saw it as a threat to his rule and ordered that all the books of Confucius should be burnt and Confucian scholars executed by being buried alive.

timeline

Mencius

Mencius is often referred to as the most famous Confucian after Confucius. By tradition he is believed to have been a disciple of the Master's grandson, Zisi. One legend tells how, as a child, Mencius moved house three times because his mother was searching for the correct environment in which he could study. Confucianism places a high premium on education. In imitation of Confucius, Mencius spent 40 years travelling about China, teaching and offering advice to rulers on how to act ethically towards their subjects.

While upholding Confucius's belief in the hierarchy of rulers and ruled, Mencius added a new thought: that if those in charge failed to act morally and treat their subjects with respect, then their subjects were justified in overthrowing them. Mencius's dealings with rulers were recorded in the Four Books, texts that were later to have a profound influence on Neo-Confucianism. In particular, their suggestion that humankind is innately good but is caused to do wrong by society saw Mencius again going beyond what his Master had taught.

Huang Di's philosophy of government embraced the then dominant ideology of legalism, a set of pragmatic principles that encouraged rulers to do what was expedient and right for them rather than in the best interests of their subjects as Confucius advocated. But it proved unpopular, and when the emperor was overthrown two decades later by the Han dynasty, Confucian principles were in the ascendant.

> **How happy it is to welcome friends from afar.**
> **Confucius** (used at the opening of the 2008 Beijing Olympics)

c.200 BCE	c.1200 BCE	1960s	2008
Han dynasty promotes Confucianism	Zhu Xi and Neo-Confucianism	Cultural Revolution	Confucian slogan at Beijing Olympics

> *He who rules his state on a moral basis would be supported by the people, just as the Polar star is encircled by all the other stars.*
>
> **Confucius**

The Han dynasty lasted until 220 CE and confirmed Confucianism as a religion by elevating Confucius to a perfection of thought and correctness that was unarguable, something to be learned, studied and ultimately worshipped.

Neo-Confucianism This elevated status persisted long after the fall of the Han dynasty, but Confucianism underwent changes along the way, most notably when, under the Song dynasty, Zhu Xi (1130–1200) offered a radical reinterpretation of Confucius's Five Classics that became the basis for what is today known as Neo-Confucianism. He brought Buddhist and Taoist influences to bear on Confucianism, partially merging the three, especially in terms of ritual and concern for the soul, though he did not embrace Buddhist

Confucian temples

The oldest and largest Confucian temple in the world is situated at Qufu, where Confucius was born and died. It was established in 478 BCE, the year after his death, and has nine courtyards. Most Confucian temples have only two or three. In line with Confucius's original inspiration, these temples are as much about education – usually including a school – as they are about worship. Unlike Buddhism, Confucianism avoids images, and so there are rarely likenesses of the Master in temples. It is Confucius's thought, rather than the man himself, that is important and venerated. On his birthday, the state-sponsored cult in China that encourages sacrifices to his spirit stages public celebrations, which include an ancient Eight Row Dance, performed by eight columns of eight dancers, dating back to ceremonies that used to honour the Chinese emperors.

notions of *karma* and reincarnation. *Life* magazine has ranked Zhu Xi as the forty-fifth most important person in the last millennium.

The role of Confucian thought in underpinning almost two millennia of autocratic rule in China made it a natural target for the Chinese Communist movement that came to power in 1949. Confucius was accused of having a 'feudal mentality'. Chairman Mao's Little Red Book was to replace Confucius's writings as the core philosophy of the nation and should be treated with the same inviolate devotion and obedience. Any person carrying a copy and loudly proclaiming its contents could expect to advance in the party ranks.

Rehabilitation Yet Confucius was not inevitably the antithesis of Communist principles. His emphasis, for example, on the good of the group or community over the rights of the individual chimed well with Communist thought, and by the 1980s he was rehabilitated in China. His birthday is now marked with ceremonies around the country, and Chinese Communist leaders regularly quote him in speeches. A popularization of his writings by a Chinese academic, Yu Dan, published in 2008, has sold more than 10 million copies, and on the campus of Beijing's prestigious Tsinghua University where there used to be a statue of Chairman Mao, there is now one of Confucius. He is, for most modern Chinese, *a junzi* – saint, scholar and 'perfect gentleman'.

That statue symbolizes the role of Confucianism as an integral part of the political, academic, social and religious fabric of modern-day China. Confucius's thoughts are still regarded by the Chinese in a religious way, even if he did not, as scholars continue to point out, aim to found a religion.

the condensed idea
Confucianism still informs the Chinese psyche

41 Taoism

Taoism has no founder or founding moment, and it venerates neither God nor gods but rather a universal principle – Tao – that it holds to be beyond words. Its core philosophy, based on ancient Chinese creeds, heavily influenced by Buddhism and originally in marked contrast to Confucianism, remains hard to define. Some of its key notions have become well known, often out of context, in the West. Principal among them are feng shui, t'ai chi and Yin Yang.

The origins of Taoism – Daoism in some translations – lie around 2,500 years ago, in the Axial Age, and coincide with the emergence of Confucianism. Taoism too grew out of the nature religions and shamanism – communicating with the spirit world – found in and around China in this period.

First anarchist Two of the key figures in the birth of Taoism are the hermit monk Zhuangzi (c.370–311 BCE) and the sixth-century BCE sage Lao Tzu. Unlike Confucius, Zhuangzi did not concern himself with governance and the relationship between ruler and ruled; in fact, he has been described as the world's first anarchist. 'Good order results spontaneously when things are let alone,' he wrote in the sacred text that is known by his name. The Zhuangzi, however, is actually an anthology of texts dating from the fourth to the end of the third century. Only its first seven chapters – the 'Inner Chapters' – are regarded as being potentially Zhuangzi's own work.

timeline

6th century BCE	c.370 BCE
Life of Lao Tzu	Birth of Zhuangzi

Lao Tzu is venerated as the author of the principal Taoist holy book, Tao Te Ching (Classic of the Way and Its Potency). However, little is known about him. His name simply means 'Old Master', and again the text appears to be a collection rather than the work of a single individual. In its 81 short chapters, written in often opaque verse, it extols the virtues of selflessness and personal searching, but it was its suggestion that rulers should intervene as little as possible in the lives of their subjects that made it appeal to the legalists, the opponents of Confucius.

T'ai chi

The association between Taoism and the ancient Chinese martial arts is explained in both Zhuangzi and Tao Te Ching. The two texts explore the psychology, practice and ethics of martial arts in line with Chinese tradition. T'ai chi is believed to have been developed as a set of spiritual exercises by the Chinese Taoist priest Zhang Sanfeng, whose dates are given as 1127–1279 CE, although some scholars question whether he too is a mythical figure. Modern forms of t'ai chi found in the West are likely to be closer to secular exercise regimes than to Taoist practices.

Celestial master A third possible date for the emergence of Taoism is 142 CE, when its first celestial master, Zhang Daoling, is said to have received a revelation from Lao Tzu, now the god-like personification of Tao itself. Zhang was a hermit monk living on Mount Heming when Lao Tzu appeared to him to tell him that the world was coming to an end and would be followed by a 'great peace'. To help others achieve this ill-defined state, Lao Tzu explained, Zhang must act as an intermediary between humankind and the celestial powers in enforcing a new covenant, which would demand a radical change in behaviour, symbolized by abandoning existing rituals. Dwelling on particular dates in history is, however, to miss the essential point of Taoism. It is not who revealed Tao that is important. It is Tao itself. In simple terms Tao can be translated as 'the way', or even 'the way of heaven', but it is

142 CE	7th century	1949
Zhang Daoling's revelation	Taoism achieves semi-official status	Banned by Chairman Mao

> **‘There was something undifferentiated and yet complete,**
> **Which existed before Heaven and Earth.**
> **Soundless and formless it depends on nothing and does not change.**
> **It operates everywhere and is free from danger.**
> **It may be considered the mother of the universe.**
> **I do not know its name; I call it Tao.’**
>
> Tao Te Ching, **6th century** BCE

much more than that. In Tao, everything in the universe is unified and connected.

Tao is not a god – though Taoism has its deities. They are part of the universe, and in the same way as everything else are therefore dependent on Tao. Tao has no being and can't be seen, though its effects are visible. It is often described as ineffable – beyond the power of words to sum up – but in any case Taoism teaches that speculating on what it is or isn't is a waste of energy; it is living it out that matters

Self-development The central concerns of Taoism are: achieving a state of harmony or union with nature; the pursuit of spiritual immortality; acting virtuously but discreetly; and above all, self-development. It is towards that last goal that Taoism's distinctive practices are geared. Meditation is encouraged – in line with Taoism's

Feng shui

Feng shui can be traced back beyond Taoism to ancient Chinese cosmology and astrology. Its close association with Taoism came about as a result of their shared principle of Yin Yang and their mutual interest in *chi* – or the energies that shape the universe. Feng shui is one of those aspects of Taoism that has been exported to the West, particularly during the time of the hippie counter-culture of the 1960s. More recently it has been reduced to a technique for ordering and aligning rooms, offices, buildings and even townscapes in line with cosmic energies.

Buddhist influences. In Taoist temples a host of gods and goddesses are worshipped, many drawn from traditional Chinese religions. The point of liturgy, however, is to allow those who attend to align themselves more closely with Tao, often with the help of priests and monks.

Yin Yang Taoism sees body and spirit as a single entity. It teaches of The One, which is the essence of Tao and the energy of life. The relationship between The One and Tao is defined as akin to that of a son to his mother. That essence is comprised of concepts such as Wu and Yu – being and non-being; Te – virtue or integrity; Tzu Jan – naturalness or spontaneity; and Wu Wei – uncontrived action or lack of action. 'When nothing is done, nothing is left undone,' says the Tao Te Ching.

Part of this pattern too is Yin Yang, which expresses another key idea in Taoism: that of opposite forces that come together to create not chaos, as in other religions, but essential harmony. Like other parts of the intricate and interconnected pattern of Taoist belief, Yin Yang is often taught separately as a non-religious discipline in the West, or combined with other New Age concepts cherry-picked from around the globe.

Persecution and flight The history of Taoism is one of a fluctuating relationship with those in authority. It achieved great influence and semi-official status under the Tang dynasty (618–907 CE) and the Song dynasty (960–1279), but that declined when Zhu Xi integrated some of its practices into Neo-Confucianism (see Chapter 40). Taoism traditionally looks up to the celestial masters, the successors of Zhang Daoling, who in recent times have been in exile in Taiwan, having been driven out of mainland China in 1949 after Chairman Mao came to power. Mao's Communist regime banned Taoism and all but wiped it out of existence, though recently it has enjoyed a revival, and there are now an estimated 20 to 50 million Taoists in the world.

the condensed idea
Live out 'the way', don't speculate on it

42 Shintoism

Shinto is the belief system subscribed to by most of the population of Japan. Its relationship with Buddhism is a complicated one. Some Japanese will embrace both Buddhism and Shinto simultaneously and see no conflict between the two. Others regard Shinto as the product of a merger between the Buddhism that came to Japan from China around the sixth century CE and an earlier, home-grown Japanese religious cult. Taking many diverse forms, Shinto has at various stages in its history been annexed to Japanese nationalism, but today it is seen very much as a personal credo for its 119 million followers.

On its journey eastwards from India to Japan, Buddhism was shaped by contact with various Chinese religions. So into the mix that made up Shinto went both Buddhism and Confucianism, with a dash of Taoism, plus the existing native creed of the Japanese. This taught of a distant deity, worshipped by the community, especially at crucial times such as harvest, and also included elements of cosmology and an ancient mythology of elaborate moral fables.

Kami At the heart of Shinto beliefs is the concept of *kami*, which translates variously as 'a god', 'gods', 'a spirit', or 'spiritual essence'. The word is best known in the West from the kamikaze pilots of the Japanese air force in the Second World War, who would sacrifice their own lives by flying their planes into targets. *Kaze* means 'wind', so kamikaze is 'divine wind'.

timeline

6th century CE	712
Buddhist monks arrive in Japan	Kojiki compiled

Shinto is not especially a belief system or an attempt to explain away the world and its suffering. It is more a spiritual intuition that *kami* is everywhere around us – in ourselves, in animals, in the seasons, in ancestors, in rivers and mountains. It amounts to a sacred element or energy here on Earth. Shinto devotion to *kami* is such that, as a faith, it is focused exclusively on this world rather than an afterlife or eternity. The supernatural is to be discovered in the here and now.

The social and cultural side of Shinto is often indistinguishable from its spiritual and ritual aspects. Some argue that it is not a distinct religion at all, but rather an aspect of Japanese life, laying down principles of ethical behaviour and conduct for the population. So the imperative to show respect at all times – often by bowing – is part of Shinto ritual.

Sacred texts Shinto prides itself on being about actions and rituals rather than words and complex theories. It does not, therefore, place too much emphasis on holy books. The first attempt at recording its history and collected insights came in 712 CE with Kojiki, 'The Record of Ancient Matters', which describes the relationship between spirits, nature and people, and includes a creation myth portraying the Japanese archipelago as a paradise fashioned by the gods as their first task on Earth.

> **To be fully alive is to have an aesthetic perception of life because a major part of the world's goodness lies in its often unspeakable beauty**
>
> **Rev Yukitaka Yamamoto:** leading Shinto priest and writer

720	1638	1860s
Nihon Shoki	Christian missionaries expelled	Meiji restoration

Missionaries in Japan

Though Shinto is tolerant of other faiths, the Christian missionary push into Japan in the middle of the sixteenth century, spearheaded by the celebrated Jesuit priest Francis Xavier, ended in failure. The Japanese had at first been willing to welcome the missionaries because they came with Western traders, but by 1597 tolerance had worn thin and 26 Franciscan friars were executed in Nagasaki. By 1638, all Christian missionaries had been expelled. They were only readmitted at the end of the nineteenth century. The real motive behind expelling them appears to have been the fear among Japan's ruling elite that Christianity would weaken their hold over the population.

Another sacred book, Nihon Shoki, 'The Chronicle of Japan', dated around 720 CE, linked Shinto to the rulers of Japan. The emperor was portrayed as the descendant of the sun goddess Amaterasu. This nationalistic element was promoted during the Meiji restoration of the 1860s, with the emperor described as the 'high priest of Shinto'. Any claim to divinity was renounced by the Japanese imperial family after defeat in the Second World War.

Jinja Shinto The principal form of Shinto is Jinja or 'Shrine' Shinto. Its focus is on the 80,000 or so public shrines in Japan, plus the countless home shrines or *kamidana*. Other strands concentrate on different sources of *kami*. Folk or Minzoku Shinto, for example, looks to the stories and legends of the spirits.

The public shrines can be great temples or groves of sacred trees, mountaintops or waterfalls. What links them is their status as holy ground, the place of *kami*. Shrines are traditionally entered via a gate

The Japanese go to Shinto shrines for life-affirming activities and Buddhist temples for death rites

Mary Pat Fisher: Living Religions (2008)

separating them from the rest of the world. These Shinto gates – or *torii* – with two uprights and two overhanging crossbars, painted orange or black, have become one of the distinctive symbols of Japan. The most famous *torri* is at the Itsukushima shrine at Miyajama, believed to date back to the sixth century, and with its foundations resting below water on the incoming tide.

Elsewhere the sacred site is fenced off from malign outside influences by *shimenawa* ropes, traditionally made of twisted straw. In the sanctuary there are areas or buildings for worship and for leaving offerings. There will also be an object or objects known as *shintai*, which symbolizes the presence of *kami*. It may be something from nature – such as a tree or a large boulder – or even something man-made such as a mirror.

Shrine rituals

The landmarks of life are marked in Shinto by visits to the local shrine. Hatsumiyamairi is when a newborn baby is placed under the protection of *kami*. For boys it takes place on the 32nd day after birth; for girls, the 33rd. The festival of Shichigosan is named after the ages of the children taking part – seven (*shichi*), five (*go*), and three (*san*). Worshippers give thanks to the gods for the children's lives so far and pray for safe and successful futures for them. Seijin Shiki, or Adults' Day, is when anyone who has in the previous year celebrated their twentieth birthday – the age of majority in Japan – can attend the shrine to give thanks. Traditional Shinto weddings, however, have declined in popularity in recent times, with only about a quarter of the population now pledging lifelong commitment at the shrine.

The concept of purification is central to Shintoism, a notion it shares with Buddhism. Thus, those visiting a shrine will begin with the ritual of *harae* – purifying themselves. Purity in Shinto is more than simply cleanliness. It is about washing away what Christians might call sin – the stains of the world beyond *kami*.

the condensed idea
Spirits can be found everywhere

43 Contemporary credos

Many of the world's great faiths emerged as we know them now during the Axial Age, between 800 and 300 BCE. Christianity and Islam came later, but drew heavily on the insights of this earlier period. Although all have adapted to changes in the secular world, and in the lives of their followers, none could be considered of modern origin. In the past two centuries, however, a number of new religious traditions have been born, some of them the cause of great controversy. Before looking at the challenges facing religion in the contemporary age, here is a brief overview of these recent arrivals.

Baha'i Islam teaches that Muhammad was God's final prophet. Shi'a Islam, however, awaits the revelation of a new imam from among Muhammad's descendants to continue a leadership line that ended in disputed circumstances in the tenth century CE. In May 1844 in Iran, stronghold of Shi'a Islam, Siyyid Ali Muhammad, a descendant of the Prophet, declared himself to be that new imam. The Bab, as he was known, claimed that he was a messenger from God, come to announce the imminent arrival of a new prophet. He was executed in 1850 by the Iranian authorities.

In 1852, one of the Bab's jailed followers, Mirza Husayn Ali, a 35-year-old nobleman, reported experiencing a vision from God in his cell that

timeline

1852

Baha'u'llah declares himself God's prophet

identified him as the new prophet. Thereafter he called himself Baha'u'llah – 'Glory of God'. The following year he was released and exiled. He spent some time living as a hermit, but attracted an increasing number of converts by his example and his writings. Some were Muslims, but the majority were from the Christian and Jewish communities of the Middle East where Baha'u'llah lived out his exile.

In his book *Seven Valleys*, he drew deeply on the Sufi mystical tradition in Islam, but elsewhere he proclaimed a message of mutual tolerance, respect for all religions, social reform and international justice that strikes a chord with modern times. His most influential collection of writings, *Kitab-I-Aqdas*, was completed shortly before his death in 1892.

Leadership of the Baha'i faith passed first to Baha'u'llah's descendants and more recently to a council, the Universal House of Justice. Shoghi Effendi, leader of Baha'i from 1921 to 1957, produced the following summary of Baha'u'llah's message to the world: 'the independent search after truth, unfettered by superstition or tradition; the oneness of the entire human race, the pivotal principle and fundamental doctrine of the faith; the basic unity of all religions; the condemnation of all forms of prejudice, whether religious, racial, class or national; the harmony which must exist between religion and science; the equality of men and women, the two wings on which the bird of humankind is able to soar'.

> It is not for him to pride himself who loveth his own country, but rather for him who loveth the whole world. The Earth is but one country and mankind its citizens.

Baha'u'llah, 1817-92

> **I can understand why Christians call us heretics. But most important, who will God call a heretic? From God's point of view, my revelation is deeply orthodox.**

Sun Myung Moon, 1977

Baha'is are enthusiastic missionaries, and have carried the teachings of Baha'u'llah around the globe. There are now six million followers, but the faith remains persecuted in Iran, where the suggestion that Muhammad was not the final prophet is regarded as blasphemous.

Haile Selassie

The Ethiopian emperor Haile Selassie (1892–1975) never commented publicly on Rastafari beliefs that he was the incarnation of God. He set aside land at Shashamane, 200 miles south of the Ethiopian capital, Addis Ababa, for the resettlement of Rastafarians who had come from overseas, and in April 1966 was greeted by huge crowds when he visited Jamaica, an occasion marked in Rastafari on April 26 as Grounation Day. Yet Haile Selassie was also titular head of the ancient Ethiopian Orthodox Church and prayed regularly in its churches. His political method was to form alliances with the West – a policy regarded with scorn by Rastafari. He was overthrown in a coup in 1974 and died in mysterious circumstances while under arrest the following year. Some Rastafarians believe he is still alive and in hiding.

Rastafari Rastafari is a creed that developed in Jamaica in the 1930s and now has an estimated one million followers worldwide. It holds that Haile Selassie, the King of Ethiopia from 1930 to 1975, was the incarnation of God, and that he will use his divine powers to return to Africa – 'the land of Zion' – members of the Afro-Caribbean community who are living in exile in the West – 'the land of Babylon' – as a result of colonization and the slave trade. Rastafarians believe that black Africans are God's chosen race.

The roots of Rastafari lie in the work of the 1930s Jamaican political activist Marcus Garvey, regarded by Rastafarians as a prophet. It has grown into a distinctive spiritual movement, based on the Old Testament texts of the Bible, which also embraces reincarnation, the

Sun Myung Moon

Sun Myung Moon was born in 1920 in Japanese-occupied Korea. His early education was Confucian, but at the age of 10 he converted to Christianity and joined the Presbyterians. He claims that at 16 he was visited by Jesus, who instructed him to complete his unfinished work of establishing God's kingdom on earth. Moon's early years as a preacher saw him jailed in what is now North Korea. In 1950 he was released by UN troops and in 1954 founded the Unification Church. All this took place against the backdrop of the Korean War (1950–3), a battle between the Communist North and the Western-backed South. In 1958 Moon sent his first missionaries to Japan and the next year to America. By 1975 his church operated in 120 countries.

ritual use of marijuana to increase spirituality, and the practice of leaving hair uncut and twisted into trademark dreadlocks.

The Moonies The Unification Church – better known as the Moonies – was established in Korea in the 1950s by Sun Myung Moon, and has around one million members worldwide. Moon claims to be the Second Coming of Christ, and maintains that he has been in contact with Confucius, Buddha and Jesus Christ. The church's belief system draws on both Christianity and Eastern faiths, and advocates the unity of all religions in order to create a heaven on Earth. It has urged Christians to abandon the crucifix as their symbol – because it reminds people of pain – and replace it with the crown. Its 'blessing ceremonies' – described by some as mass weddings of couples matched by Moon – remain controversial, as does the founder himself. In 1982 he was convicted of tax fraud in the United States.

the condensed idea
There are always new ways to God

44 Religion and science

The relationship between religion and science has long been a fraught one. Religion is concerned with faith, science with proof. No mainstream religions claim to be able to 'prove' in the empirical terms favoured by science the existence of a deity, but nevertheless they believe in one (or several). Some scientists – notably Richard Dawkins, the evolutionary biologist – react to this by claiming that faith therefore is not soundly or rationally based and has no place in the modern world.

Religion and science did once have much more common ground – and continue to do so in some faith traditions. Buddhism, for instance, rejects hostility to science and encourages the impartial investigation of creation, not least of humankind itself. A central tenet of Baha'i is that religion and science need to be in harmony: religion without science is superstition, and science without religion is materialism.

Faith and reason Throughout the history of religion there have been periods where there was no perceived division between faith and reason. The exploration of nature, for instance, was applauded in the thirteenth century in Thomas Aquinas's *Summa Theologica*. Between the eighth and fourteenth centuries there was a flourishing of scientific exploration under Islam. Algebra, algorithms and alkalis were all discovered at this time, and remain at the very heart of mathematics, physics, computer science and chemistry. Hinduism too encouraged

timeline

*c.*1000 BCE	8th to 14th centuries
Vedic arithmetic	Islamic Golden Age

Islam and science

Between the eighth and fourteenth centuries, an era that is now often referred to as 'Islam's Golden Age', scholars working in Islamic lands made a great contribution to the world's understanding of science. Their inspiration, it is believed, was a verse from the Qur'an – 'He has taught you what you did not know' – which they interpreted as encouraging the acquisition of knowledge. In the fields of astrology, geography and mathematics important advances were made, including the development of algebra, which was prompted, it was said, by the need to make sense of Islamic inheritance laws.

mathematics: operations including squares, cubes and roots are all to be found in sacred Vedic texts dating back to 1000 BCE.

Well into the medieval period, Christianity continued to regard science as a subsidiary branch of religion and worked to synthesize its discoveries with the teachings of the Church. That endeavour, however, became progressively more difficult and raised the issue that still stands at the heart of the dispute between religion and science – namely that the two use very different methodologies. On one side there is what is revealed to believers; on the other what is observable by scientists.

Galileo Galilei The most prominent victim of the falling-out between religion and science was the Tuscan physicist, mathematician and astronomer Galileo Galilei (1564–1642), who is today often called 'the father of modern science'. Galileo was a Christian and a friend of popes, but he came under attack because he spoke out publicly about how the Earth revolved around a stationary sun. The Church, taking its lead from the Old Testament, officially rejected this position, though many senior figures privately accepted that Galileo was right.

1633
Galileo faces the Inquisition

1859
Origin of Species

2006
The God Delusion

> **Just as the feathers of a peacock and the jewel-stone of a snake are placed at the highest point of the body, so is the position of mathematics the highest amongst all branches of the Vedas and the Shastras.**
>
> **Vedang Jyotish (Vedic text),** *c.*1000 BCE

In 1633, he was summoned before the Inquisition, forced to recant his views and placed under house arrest for the remainder of his life. His writings were banned until 1718, and remained on the Church's Index of Forbidden Books until 1835. In 1992, however, Pope John Paul II, in the course of encouraging a new working relationship between religion and science, made a public statement of regret for the way in which the Church had treated Galileo.

Enlightenment The gulf between religion and science grew wider with the Scientific Enlightenment of the eighteenth century. In 1859, Charles Darwin published his *On the Origin of Species*, arguing for the evolution over time of all life forms on Earth from common ancestors on the basis of natural selection, or the survival of the fittest. This stood in direct contravention of the creation story in the Book of Genesis, and earned him the vocal hostility of Christianity.

One of Darwin's most vociferous critics was the Anglican Bishop of Oxford, Samuel Wilberforce. In a famous debate in Oxford in 1860, attended by a crowd of over a thousand, Wilberforce clashed with Thomas Huxley, a biologist and close associate of Darwin. Was it through his grandfather or his grandmother, Wilberforce asked Huxley, that he was descended from a monkey? Huxley replied that he was not ashamed to have a monkey as an ancestor, but he was ashamed of his connection with a man such as Wilberforce who used his gifts to obscure the truth.

Darwin himself, not one to dismiss religion, avoided such face-to-face confrontations. He commented: 'It appears to me (whether rightly or wrongly) that direct arguments against Christianity and theism produce hardly any effect on the public; and freedom of thought is best promoted by the gradual illumination of men's minds which follows from the advance of science.'

Integration or independence?

The twentieth century saw the start of a rapprochement. The French Jesuit and palaeontologist Father Pierre Teilhard de Chardin (1881–1955) attempted to synthesize the theory of evolution with the account in the Book of Genesis of the world's creation by God. Religion and science could, he believed, be integrated.

At least three other distinctive approaches exist regarding religion and science: dialogue, independence and conflict. Dialogue has seen clerics, theologians and scientists gather round the same table to explore their differences. Around 40 per cent of scientists are estimated to hold some sort of religious belief. Independence is the acceptance that religion and science exist in what the American evolutionary biologist Stephen Jay Gould (1941–2002) labelled 'non-overlapping magisteria' – in other words that they are concerned with completely separate aspects of human existence. Conflict is epitomized by *The God Delusion* (2006), the best-selling out-and-out attack on religion by the Oxford-based scientist Professor Richard Dawkins. Belief in a personal God, he wrote, was a kind of madness, but a delusion that had persisted in spite of all the evidence to the contrary. In laying out that evidence, he accuses organized religion of impeding the progress of science.

Studies of the efficacy of prayer

If there is a God, scientists have suggested, then praying to that God should show some measurable effects. There has been much research into this proposition, but with few clear conclusions. One of the first to run a test was the Victorian intellectual Sir Francis Galton, who in 1872 argued that since the British royal family was regularly commended to God in prayers by its loyal subjects, its members should outlive the rest of society. Since this did not happen, he concluded, prayer did not work. Subsequent research programmes on 'third-party prayer' – praying for someone who is ill – have shown a wide variety of results in terms of the patients' outcomes. Efforts to assess scientifically the effects of faith healers have detected no proof that they achieve their stated purpose, but the widely reported 2001 Bernardi survey did indicate that believers with heart problems could improve their blood pressure by praying or reciting yoga mantras.

the condensed idea
Religion and science remain poles apart

45 Atheism

Atheism has traditionally been seen simply as the rejection of religion, but with the onward march of secular, scientific philosophies, especially in Western society, it is now regarded by some as a religion in its own right, offering God-free rituals to mark birth, marriage and death. Some 2.3 per cent of the world's population describes itself as atheist.

For as long as there have been people worshipping a deity, there have been other people disagreeing with them. The rapid growth in atheism to its current high point can, though, be more accurately dated back to the nineteenth century and philosophers such as Friedrich Nietzsche (1844–1900), who proclaimed unambiguously that 'God is dead'. He first made the remark in *The Gay Science* of 1882, but it is best known from his classic four-part philosophical novel *Thus Spoke Zarathustra* (1883–5).

The word 'atheism' breaks into two component Greek parts – *a*, meaning 'without', and *theism*, 'belief in god(s)'. It is possible, however, to be atheist *and* religious, depending on your definition. Buddhists, for instance, eschew any notion of a personal god, while there are many Jews who are without religious faith. The celebrated novelist Graham Greene (1904–91) was fond of describing himself as a Catholic who didn't believe in God.

Out with the pantheon Attempts to find a starting date for atheism usually focus on Greek and Roman philosophers, who – while not entirely rejecting their society's attachment to gods – argued

timeline

6th century BCE	5th century BCE
Carvaka atheists	Diagoras, 'father of atheism'

passionately that these pantheons were utterly irrelevant to the state and well-being of humankind. Three founding atheists in particular are often quoted: Epicurus, Diagoras and Lucretius.

Epicurus (341–270 BCE) lived in Athens and taught that while the universe was infinite and eternal, good and bad in the world should be defined only by what gave each individual pleasure or pain. Death, he argued, was the end for both the body and the soul. Fellow Athenian Diagoras (fifth century BCE) spoke out against Greek attachment to the gods and as a result was driven from the city. He is sometimes called 'the father of atheism'. And the Roman poet and philosopher Lucretius (99–55 BCE) rejected all manifestations of the supernatural as pointless superstition.

The persecution of atheists

Diagoras was arguably the world's first persecuted atheist, chased out of Athens for rejecting the gods. Up to the seventeenth century, 'atheist' was used only as a term of abuse, and no one would freely claim to be one. By the eighteenth century, though, it had become something of a badge of honour for radicals. The poet Percy Bysshe Shelley (1792–1822) was expelled from Oxford University after publishing a pamphlet entitled 'The Necessity of Atheism', and Charles Bradlaugh (1833–1890) was continually denied his seat in the House of Commons, despite winning repeated elections, because he refused to swear an oath to God. Finally, in 1886, after six years, he was allowed to affirm the parliamentary oath, rather than swearing it on a Bible.

Hindu and Muslim atheists The Carvaka school of thought in Vedic India in the sixth century BCE was arguably the first organized atheist group within any major religion – though of course it did not use the term. Its influence was limited – it is not, for instance, counted among the six great schools of Hindu philosophy – but it is believed to have made an impact on the Buddhist position on the absence of a personal god. Carvaka's teachings – that death was the end, that sensual

> **❝Religion is the sigh of the oppressed creature, the feelings of a heartless world, just as it is the spirit of unspiritual conditions. It is the opium of the people.❞**
>
> **Karl Marx, 1843**

pleasure was a legitimate goal of humankind, and that religion had been invented – carry a distinctive echo of contemporary atheism.

In Islam, atheism is regarded as a form of rejection of Allah, the equivalent of embracing another religion. The Qur'an regards this with displeasure. 'Those who believe, then reject faith, then believe (again) and (again) reject faith, and go on increasing in unbelief, Allah will not forgive them nor guide them on the way.' Yet elsewhere it states: 'Let there be no compulsion in religion.' The Hadith is more explicit: 'Kill whoever changes his religion.' Rejecting Islam (whether for another faith or for atheism) continues to be seen in a number of Muslim countries, including Saudi Arabia, Afghanistan, Iran and Yemen, as apostasy and therefore punishable by death.

Historical Jesus It was in late eighteenth- and nineteenth-century Europe, spurred on by the Enlightenment and the burgeoning of scientific enquiry, that atheism grew into something recognizable in our own times. The German theologian D.F. Strauss was amongst that first raft of scholars to study the Bible as history rather than sacred scripture. He scandalized Christian Europe in 1835 with his biography of a strictly

The world's first atheist country

In 1967 the Marxist leader of Albania, Enver Hoxha (1908–1985), declared his country the world's first atheist state. Churches and mosques were closed, clergy arrested and tortured, and believers persecuted. His regime was supported by Communist China but shunned by most other countries. With the collapse of Communism, Albania's population has resumed religious worship in large numbers.

> **❝I will call no being good, who is not what I mean when I apply that epithet to my fellow creatures, and if such a being can sentence me to hell for not so calling him, to hell I will go.❞**
>
> **John Stuart Mill, 1872**

'historical Jesus', whose divine nature he denied. The gospel miracles, he claimed, could be explained by natural phenomena.

It is Nietzsche, though, whose influence has been most enduring. His claim that 'God is dead' prefaced his description of a time of 'nihilism' when notions of truth would no longer exist, legal codes based on the Judaeo-Christian ideals that shape European society would collapse, and nothing would have any significance.

Alongside Nietzsche's philosophical template for atheism, Charles Darwin was busy providing a rebuttal to the claim that God or gods could be seen at work in – or even as part of – creation and the natural world. 'Darwin made it possible to be an intellectually fulfilled atheist,' Richard Dawkins has written. Darwin's theory of evolution left no space for a divine creator. He sought to demonstrate how over millennia, processes of genetic variation and selection had resulted in new forms of life appearing, with others becoming extinct.

Sigmund Freud (1856–1939) meanwhile provided a psychological view that supported atheism. 'Religion,' he claimed, 'is a mass-delusion that reshaped reality to provide a certainty of happiness and a protection from suffering.'

With such comprehensive scientific underpinning, Karl Marx was able to develop a political philosophy hostile to religion, claiming that it provided emotional distraction for those at the bottom of the economic and social scale from the real problems that oppressed them.

the condensed idea
Atheism is a faith

46 Stewards of creation

Since the origins of religion are to be found in creation myths and the worship of nature gods, the perceived threat to the planet posed by climate change has come greatly to preoccupy the world's faiths in recent times. With their community networks, international reach and ethical agendas, religions are well placed to act as good stewards of creation. Implicit and explicit in many of their beliefs is the sort of radical transformation in lifestyle needed to avoid what scientists warn could be environmental catastrophe.

At the heart of most religions are stories of how the planet came about. Many are linear, as in the account, sacred to both Christianity and Judaism, of God creating the world in six days and fashioning man and woman to inhabit a paradise garden. Buddhism, however, sees creation as cyclical, and this influences its approach to questions of climate change. It has no time for a creator god to explain the origin of the universe. Instead, it teaches that everything is interdependent. What is happening now is caused in part by past events, and in its turn influences future events.

Along with other religions to emerge from the Vedic tradition and embrace reincarnation, Buddhism teaches of a series of epochs, with the world coming into being, surviving for a time, destroying itself, and then being reborn. In Buddhism in particular, this happens naturally –

timeline

c.1500 BCE	1990
Rig Veda on creation	WCC tackles climate change

> ❛Then was neither non-existence nor existence:
> there was no realm of air, no sky beyond it.
>
> Death was not then, nor was there anything immortal:
> no sign was there, the Day's and Night's divider.
> Darkness there was: at first concealed in darkness
> this All was indiscriminated chaos. All that existed
> then was void and formless: by the great power of
> Warmth was born that One.❜

Rig Veda, *c.*1500 BCE

that is, without the intervention of gods, and often as a result of human behaviour.

Creation myths Creation myths fall into two categories: those that present the planet as being created by a divine force for the benefit of humankind, and those that describe it as being for the mutual benefit of every living thing. The contrast is at its most extreme between older animist traditions such as Shinto that see spirits in trees, mountains and springs, and the younger Christian and Islamic faiths, which traditionally have regarded the rest of creation as being there to sustain humans.

This divergence of belief is what lies behind differences between the faiths regarding the treatment of animals. So Jains believe that animals and plants are the equals of human beings in that all contain living souls and should therefore be treated with respect and compassion. Jains are strict vegetarians and have for centuries organized their diet so as to reduce the human drain on world resources. In Islam, by contrast, the Qur'an instructs that animals have been created for the benefit of humankind. They should be treated kindly, but can be

Muhammad and the animals

Accounts of Muhammad's life give examples of his concern for animals. When one of the party travelling with him takes some eggs from a bird's nest, the Prophet rebukes him and insists that he return them. Asked if Allah rewards acts of charity to animals he replies: 'Yes, there is a reward for acts of charity to every beast alive.' Elsewhere he says: 'Whoever kills a sparrow or anything bigger than that without a just cause, Allah will hold him accountable on the Day of Judgment.' Just cause, though, includes wanting to eat the animal.

plundered. 'It is God who provided for you all manner of livestock, that you may ride on some of them and from some you may derive your food. And other uses in them for you to satisfy your heart's desires. It is on them, as on ships, that you make your journeys.'

Fresh challenge The challenge of finding new ways to promote ecodiversity and the survival of the planet has brought into sharp focus these differing attitudes to creation. What all religions do share is their opposition to materialism, the stockpiling of wealth and overconsumption. They therefore have common cause with environmental campaigners in arguing for changed patterns of human behaviour in relation to the planet.

> The image we have of ourselves is reflected in the way we treat the creation. If we believe that we are no more than consumers, then we shall seek fulfilment in consuming the whole Earth; but if we believe we are made in the image of God, we shall act with care and compassion, striving to become what we are created to be.

Ecumenical Patriarch Bartholomew of Constantinople, 2009

Pope Benedict and the green agenda

In April 2007, Pope Benedict XVI addressed a Vatican conference on climate change. Abuse of the environment is against God's will, he said, urging bishops, scientists and politicians to promote 'sustainable development'. Environmental protection and feeding the world's poor – long a particular concern of many religions – have sometimes been seen as conflicting issues. Christianity in particular has been accused of neglecting impending ecological disaster because of its concern with development and its opposition to controlling the birth rate through wide availability of contraceptives. However, Pope Benedict rejected the idea that there was any clash, urging 'research and promotion of lifestyles and models of production and consumption that respect creation and the real demands of sustainable progress of peoples' and urging a new attitude of responsibility for the fate of the planet: 'For environment ... read creation. The mastery of man over creation must not be despotic or senseless. Man must cultivate and safeguard God's creation.'

Religious leaders have been prominent in the campaign on climate change. The pan-Protestant World Council of Churches in Geneva was among the first, setting up a department in 1990 to investigate climate change. In the summer of 2007, international leaders from the Muslim, Jewish, Buddhist and Christian traditions gathered for a silent 'prayer for the planet' alongside a retreating Greenland glacier, while in 2008, 1,000 delegates drawn from senior figures from many faiths came to Uppsala in Sweden to sign a manifesto committing their religions to press world political leaders to make a 40 per cent cut in carbon emissions before 2020, with the burden falling disproportionately on the richer developed nations. 'Our faith traditions provide a basis for hope,' they stated, 'and reasons for not giving up ... despite our shortcomings.'

the condensed idea
We have neglected creation

47 The just war

It is frequently claimed that religion is at the heart of all the conflicts in the world. This belief is a major factor in turning people away from institutional religion. Often, however, it is the behaviour of zealots on the fringes of the faiths that is at the root of the problem. The majority of believers maintain that it is 'bad religion' that causes conflict. 'Good religion' is generally opposed to war, as the sacred scriptures make plain. And amongst those faiths that allow that in some circumstances war can be justified, the list of situations in which this applies has grown shorter and shorter with the development of modern means of combat and weapons of mass destruction.

Some traditions embrace non-violence totally. The Buddhist scriptures advise: 'In times of war, give rise in yourself to the mind of compassion, helping living beings abandon the will to fight.' The Tibetan leader, the Dalai Lama (exiled since the Chinese annexed his homeland, and the winner of the Nobel Peace Prize), continually demonstrates in word and deed Buddha's commitment to peace with his non-violent approach to the Chinese.

Ahimsa Others religions are more ambiguous. Hinduism condemns the violence of war in a tenet known by the Sanskrit word *ahimsa* – 'do no violence'. (The concept is shared with Buddhism and Jainism, though their understanding of it is slightly different.) Yet at the same time, high up in the Hindu caste system are the Kshatriyas, the warrior caste. Equally, though Guru Nanak promoted peace, and many modern Sikhs are pacifists, Sikhism has over the centuries responded to the

timeline

*c.*1500 BCE	426
Rig Veda on soldiers' morality	Augustine on just war

The right to self-defence

Many Buddhists refuse to take up arms, even to defend their own lives. Monks may use martial arts for self-defence, but can never kill another human being. In Buddhism a story is shared from the Vietnam War (1959–75). The celebrated Vietnamese Zen Buddhist monk Thich Nhat Hanh (nominated by Martin Luther King in 1967 for the Nobel Peace Prize) was challenged about his commitment throughout the conflict to non-violence. 'What if someone had wiped out all the Buddhists in the world and you were the last one left. Would you not try to kill the person who was trying to kill you, and in doing so save Buddhism?' Thich Nhat Hanh replied: 'It would be better to let him kill me. If there is any truth to Buddhism and the *dharma*, it will not disappear from the face of the Earth, but will reappear when seekers of truth are ready to rediscover it. In killing I would be betraying and abandoning the very teachings I would be seeking to preserve. So it would be better to let him kill me and remain true to the spirit of the *dharma*.'

aggression of others who would deny it freedom to worship by producing accomplished soldiers.

In trying to square the circle of being essentially peace-loving with retaining the capacity to repel aggressors, Sikhism drew up a set of principles for a 'just war' known as the Dharam Yudh. To be legitimate, a conflict must be: (1) the last resort after all other means have failed; (2) not motivated by revenge or enmity; (3) pursued with minimum force and without looting or harming civilians; and (4) concluded by all property taken, including annexed territories, being returned.

1187
Saladin spares his prisoners

17th century
Sikh Dharam Yudh

1965
Paul VI, 'No More War'

> **'No one is my enemy**
> **No one is a foreigner**
> **With all I am at peace**
> **God within us renders us**
> **Incapable of hate and prejudice.'**
>
> **Guru Nanak**

Just war Such checklists are common. In the Rig Veda, Hinduism lays down criteria for soldiers to behave morally in conflict. They must not poison the tip of their arrow, target the sick, the old, women and children, or attack from behind. Christianity too has a formulation for a 'just war'.

In the New Testament, Jesus gives differing messages about whether it can ever be right to resort to violence to solve conflicts. In Matthew's gospel (5:39), he warns: 'I say this to you: offer the wicked man no resistance. On the contrary, if anyone hits you on the right cheek, offer the other as well.' But this pacifist impulse is checked later (Luke 22:36) when he tells his followers: 'But now, if you have a purse take it; if you have a haversack, do the same; if you have no sword, sell your cloak and buy one.'

In *The City of God* (426 CE), St Augustine set out the Christian theory about just war. The aggression being confronted must be 'lasting, grave, and certain'. All other means to stop it must have failed. There must be serious prospects of success. And finally the use of arms must not produce evils and disorders graver than the evil to be eliminated.

The just war in Islam

Many Muslims object to contemporary assumptions about Islam as fundamentally warlike and unconcerned about the consequences of conflict for the innocent. Such a picture has been widespread since the deaths of almost 3,000 people in the destruction of the Twin Towers in 2001 by Islamic fanatics. Mainstream Muslims deny that uninhibited violence is part of their history and point to a longer tradition within Islam of reluctance in embarking on warfare, and of humanity in its conduct. When Saladin recaptured Jerusalem from Christian Crusaders in 1187, he found that a number of holy Muslim places had been violated, yet he forbade acts of vengeance. Those residents of the city who were caught up in the battle were taken prisoner, but released on the payment of a token ransom.

> **Violence and arms can never resolve the problems of the world.**
>
> **Pope John Paul II, 2003**

While in the past these criteria have been used to endorse campaigns of aggression that sought both to annex land and to force conversions – for example, the Crusades – today the presumption in modern Catholicism is against war. Some theologians argue that the advent of nuclear arsenals with huge destructive power makes it impossible for the final criterion for a just war ever to be met. Pope Paul VI, in an historic address to the United Nations in 1965, appealed: 'war no more, war never again!' while Pope John Paul II condemned the first Gulf War in 1991 on no fewer than 56 separate occasions, later describing the 2003 invasion of Iraq as 'a defeat for humanity'.

Islam   Perhaps the most scrutinized of the religious traditions in relation to war of late has been Islam, as a result of terrorist atrocities carried out by Islamic extremists. Islam does allow war for 'noble' motives, namely self-defence and to protect oppressed Muslims in another country. It insists that non-combatants should not be injured, and that the minimum necessary force be used, with humane treatment of prisoners of war. All of these teachings are based on passages in the Qur'an and on Muhammad's own conduct.

There is dispute, however, over the so-called 'sword verses' of the Qur'an, which permit war only in self-defence and never as a means of spreading Islam. Some radical thinkers argue that the perceived hostility that Islam faces in the modern world, especially from the West, demands self-defence. Whatever the case, the Qur'an teaches that there can be no earthly reward for warfare. If it has been fought for the right reasons, Allah will judge, and the reward will be in heaven.

the condensed idea
War can rarely if ever be justified today

48 The missionary impulse

Many religions embrace the missionary spirit. The imperative to go out and evangelize is deep-rooted among those who want to share their beliefs with as many people as possible. Yet it can also be amongst the most controversial religious activity – both in past times and today. In sub-Saharan Africa, for instance, tensions between Christian and Muslim communities have been exacerbated by efforts on both sides to win – or sometimes force – conversions.

The Bible's instruction 'go ye therefore and teach all nations' has been fundamental to Christianity from its inception. Islam too was spread rapidly across north Africa and into Spain in the years immediately after Muhammad's death, while the travelling monks of Buddhism carried their beliefs into China, Tibet and Japan.

All embraced peaceful means and eschewed forced conversion. Yet when religion was inextricably linked with political power – in Christian Europe, in the Islamic caliphate and in China when Confucianism and Taoism were both taken up by the ruling dynasties – the choice of whether or not to convert, or embrace as Islam prefers to put it, carried with it consequences for daily life.

For those who rejected Islam in the territories of the caliphate, there were taxes to be paid, but broadly tolerance. For the pagans and Jews

timeline

1st century CE	5th century CE
Christ's apostles spread 'Good News'	Buddhist monks go on mission to China

who remained outside Christainity as the alliance of Holy Roman Emperor and Pope swept across Europe, there was in medieval times persecution and the Inquisition. And in China, if the Emperor favoured Taoism, Confucians would be targeted, and, on occasion, vice versa.

New World The Spanish Catholic priests and nuns who accompanied the Conquistadors into the 'New World' following the arrival there of Christopher Columbus in 1492 confronted a problem that has dogged missionaries ever since. They were with evident sincerity bringing God to indigenous peoples, often sweeping away existing belief patterns as a result, but for the conquered peoples they were also part of the subjugation . Some – like Bartoleme de las Casas, the Spanish priest known as the 'Defender of the Indians' because he objected to the way the early Spanish colonial authorities treated native peoples as slaves – insisted that religion could not have two standards, one for the conquerors and one for the conquered, but many were not so scrupulous. Conversion to Christianity was used as a tool for making the local population – and the slaves imported from Africa – more submissive.

Catholicism, nevertheless, took firm hold in the Spanish Empire, now Latin and Central America, though it did not entirely displace existing religions. The result was syncretism – the mixing of two different beliefs – which continues to dog missionary efforts in many areas of the world to this day. In Brazil, for instance – colonized by the Portuguese on much the same principles as those employed by the Spanish – Candomble thrives alongside Catholicism, sharing the same followers.

If a commission by an earthly king is considered an honour, how can a commission by a Heavenly King be considered a sacrifice?

David Livingstone, 1813–73

7th century CE
Muhammad's disciples export Islam

1492
'Discovery' of the Americas

19th century
High point of European missionary activity

Santaria

Santaria is another of the syncretic religions that developed at the time of the European colonization of the Americas. Its strongest base today is Cuba, but it has a substantial number of followers in the United States. A mixture of Catholic, African and Native American beliefs, Santaria teaches of a single god, Obatala, above all the other deities, or *orishas*. Its rituals include exorcism and animal sacrifice, and it has been linked to voodoo. In the past, the Catholic Church and the colonial authorities attempted to stamp it out, so Santaria developed a system of naming its *orishas* after Christian saints so as to keep their real identities secret. The Santaria god of the sick, Babalu-Aye, for instance, is also known as St Lazarus.

A mixture of ancient African rites and rituals brought over by slaves, and elements of Catholicism, it counts around two million adherents and is centred on the north-eastern city of Salvador da Bahia.

Most modern societies respect as a fundamental human right the freedom of individuals to choose what to believe, but that has not put an end to missionary work. The mainstream religions today work in public and in private to promote mutual understanding and respect, yet they still seek to make converts.

Peaceful co-existence Not all religions follow this pattern. Judaism does have a formal process for conversion but recoils from the zeal for mass evangelization of some branches of the other two monotheistic faiths, Christianity and Islam. This is the result of a history of attempts by other faiths to forcibly convert Jews.

Meanwhile some religions do not demand exclusivity from their followers and can cope with adherents having other allegiances simultaneously. Within Christianity, the Baptists accept that those attending their services may retain links to other denominations. The Baha'i, among the most successful missionaries of recent times, recognize as part of the absolute respect they show to all religions that converts will often keep a foot in more than one camp. And Shinto in Japan co-exists peacefully in many lives with Buddhism, with some Japanese choosing, for example, a Shinto ceremony for baptism and a Buddhist one for funerals.

The spirit of self-sacrifice

Whatever the ethics of their desire to make converts, the missionaries who accompanied European colonizers undoubtedly had courage and a willingness to die for their faith. Some would carry their personal belongings and quantities of Bibles and hymn books in coffin-shaped suitcases. They anticipated dying on the job, and many did so, either through disease, or – for an unfortunate few – as martyrs at the hands of those they had gone to save. Such a fate, however, was seen in the militant missionary mindset as 'God working out his purpose', in the title of the classic 1894 missionary hymn.

Flashpoints The missionary impulse, however, continues to cause conflict. In India, the activity of Christian missionaries is deeply resented by many Hindus, who believe that their efforts to attract converts are destroying the national fabric of India. In recent times this resentment has erupted into violence, with Hindu leaders accusing Christian missionaries of denigrating their gods. In one well-publicized incident in January 1999, an Australian Christian missionary, Graham Staines, and his two young sons were burnt alive in the state of Orissa while they slept in their camper van. He had been accused of proselytizing.

A source of particular disquiet has been the activity of new churches and groups on the fundamentalist fringes of the mainstream faiths – again, notably Christianity and Islam – which have worked openly to encourage mass conversion. Some Islamic groups in European countries, for instance, have the stated purpose of boosting the Muslim populations there to enable the creation of Islamic states, run on the principles of Shar'iah law. Mainstream Muslims reject such an approach, and seek instead to promote tolerance and understanding between faith groups.

the condensed idea
I want all to believe the same as me

49 Spirituality

The world economic downturn of 2008–9 may have caused a crisis of faith in capitalism and consumerism, but according to some accounts, it has inspired a revival of interest in religion, especially in Western society. This has manifested itself not in an upturn in attendance at churches, mosques and temples, but instead in high levels of demand for retreats, meditation courses and workshops, places where participants are instructed in the sort of tools traditionally used by faiths to access what is broadly but vaguely called spirituality.

Spirituality and religion are often treated as synonymous, but they are not. Religion might be better seen as one way to access the spiritual. Alternatively it is an external, communal format for spirituality, in contrast to other more internal, individualistic manifestations that can be accessed via various forms of introspection – meditation, contemplation of nature, or achieving a heightened state of awareness through fasting or other bodily disciplines.

Christianity, Islam and Judaism all have their particular spiritual traditions, as has been detailed in previous chapters. Each attempts a more intimate, personal and mystical relationship with the divine than is found in the usual rites and rituals. Some are more integrated at the heart of their faith tradition than others. Sufism, for instance, is arguably more acceptable to mainstream Muslims than Kabbalah is to mainstream Jews. Christianity, meanwhile, has a long history of regarding with suspicion, certainly within their lifetimes, those who

timeline

3rd century CE	1515
Hermit monks of Christianity go into desert	Birth of St Teresa of Avila

emphazise the spiritual side of the faith over and above conventional liturgy, rules and structures.

St Teresa of Avila

The Spanish Carmelite St Teresa of Avila (1515–82) is a case in point. As a young nun in her enclosed convent, she devoted herself to introspection and contemplative prayer, and finally reached, according to her spiritual autobiography, *The Interior Castle*, states of religious ecstasy in which she felt herself at one with God. She recommended a fourfold spiritual path so that others could follow in her footsteps. It started with 'mental prayer' that shut out the world, stepped up to 'prayer of quiet', where she lost herself in God, built to 'devotion of union', where she reached an ecstatic state, and finally arrived at 'devotion of ecstasy', a trance-like state in which her senses ceased to work and her body felt as if it was floating.

Silence

In recent times, Western monasteries of both the monotheistic and the Eastern religions have reported a surge in enquiries from spiritually hungry visitors wanting to sample a life of contemplation and silence. Church leaders also extol the virtues of silence as a cure for economic and ecological uncertainties. Rowan Williams, the monk-like Archbishop of Canterbury who leads the Anglican Communion, has spoken of 'the realm of silence' as a 'crucial part of the daily discipline'. The ancient lifestyle of hermits, once central to the early Christian Church and still a feature of Eastern traditions, is likewise undergoing a revival in interest. Silence is prized as creating a complete atmosphere that promotes spirituality and interiority. Most religions regard it as a kind of presence, rather than the absence of something. So by not talking, individuals are enabled to find themselves at a deeper spiritual level.

Yet in her lifetime, many people believed that Teresa's trances were actually an indication that she was possessed by the devil. Her fellow nuns often criticized and sidelined her, and when she sought to reform

> **Contemplative prayer in my opinion is nothing else than a close sharing between friends; it means taking time frequently to be alone with him who we know loves us.**
>
> St Teresa of Avila

the order, to make it less worldly and more geared to the spiritual life, she faced obstacles at every turn. Like many supremely spiritual figures in Christianity, she has been more appreciated in death – she is now one of only a handful of female 'Doctors of the Church' – than she ever was in life.

Body and spirit By contrast, in Eastern religious traditions, that division between religion and spirituality scarcely exists. In some – for example, the Jains – the self-sacrifice of monks and nuns is held to enable them to access a higher level of spiritual awareness than the majority of believers, who have also to contend with the everyday details of family and work. Buddhism, however, encourages everyone – monk or not – to meditate, believing that it is a mental and physical

Bede Griffiths

The British-born Benedictine monk Bede Griffiths (1906–93) spent much of his adult life living in the ashrams of southern India, attempting to make a synthesis between Western Christianity and Eastern spirituality. Although he remained a Catholic monk, he adopted the trappings of Hindu monastic life and entered into a dialogue with Hinduism that he chronicled in 12 popular books.

One key concept for him was 'integral thought' – the attempt to harmonize spiritual and scientific world views. 'We're now being challenged,' he wrote in 1983, 'to create a theology which would use the findings of modern science and Eastern mysticism which coincide so much, and to evolve from that a new theology which would be much more adequate.'

> **❝Silence is our first human language. Solitude should be in everyone's life – not as a permanent exterior condition but as an internalised monastery. Then we can live in the world with calm harmony.❞**
> **Revd Cynthia Bourgeault, 2009**

discipline that will allow them to separate themselves from their thoughts and feelings and thus reach a higher state of consciousness. Meditation isn't something apart from the everyday life or ritual practice of a Buddhist. It is at the heart of it.

In Taoism too there is an emphasis on overcoming the division between body and spirit. It teaches that physical actions have spiritual effects, and so followers engage their bodies in practices such as t'ai chi in order to create the mental space to know the Tao directly. Bodily purity (by, for example, following a strict diet) is inextricably linked to spiritual health.

East–West traffic Eastern perspectives on enhancing spirituality have long been influential in the West. The Transcendalist movement in the United States and Europe in the nineteenth century was profoundly influenced by Vedic and Hindu thought. It emphasized the importance of accessing an inner track or core of spiritual thought and a relationship with the divine that had little to do with institutions of religion.

In more recent times, various popular 'New Age' spiritual movements have borrowed aspects of Eastern rituals and practice, though these are sometimes annexed without their original context. Taoism's Yin Yang and feng shui, for example, have become in Western hands lifestyle choices, all but denuded of religious significance, rather than part of a faith tradition.

the condensed idea
Body and spirit can work as one

50 The future of religion

The confident prediction that religion has had its day, heard ever louder since the nineteenth century, has proved premature. Even if the focus is on Europe alone, where numbers of believers have undeniably dropped, God is not dead. Religion at the start of the twenty-first century may be changing, but it shows no sign of fading away. Indeed, around the globe, in Africa, Asia and Latin America, the numbers of those claiming a formal religious allegiance are on the up.

There is a negative viewpoint on all this that sees adherence to religion only in terms of the security blanket it allegedly provides for people who fear for themselves and ultimately for the end of the world. According to those who subscribe to this perspective, religion is surviving and flourishing only because the world is in such a mess. Scientists tell us that the planet is facing environmental disaster. The divide between rich and poor nations grows wider despite all our attempts to close it. And notwithstanding the efforts of science, the randomness of suffering continues to puzzle us.

That God-shaped hole One of the great objections to organized religion in the West has long been the political and social power it commands. The French philosopher Jean-Paul Sartre (1905–80) used the phrase 'a God-shaped hole' to describe that place in the human

timeline

1882
Nietzsche declares God is dead

2006
Worldwide Catholic population grows to 1.2 billion

consciousness where God has always been. Yet he argued that we must reject God and leave the hole empty because religion negates personal freedom and liberty. It is, in short, too tarnished by its attempts, often hand-in-hand with political power, to make us conform to its will.

Yet the era of Church and state jointly shaping lives in their own image with God's blessing appears to be over, certainly in Europe and increasingly in the United States. The objections raised by Christian teaching, and articulated plainly and often angrily by Christian leaders, to homosexual relationships, contraception, sex outside marriage and, above all others, abortion, seen by many believers as the keystone test of morals and ethics, have been overruled by legislators and increasingly by public opinion.

Fundamentalism Where does that leave religion, especially in the West? The material and the spiritual, God and Mammon, continue to overlap, but not to the same extent as previously. Many believers regard such a development as a positive thing, an opportunity for religion to return to serving humanity, rather than coercing it.

Paul Tillich

The German-born American theologian and philosopher Paul Tillich (1868–1965) argued that religion was necessary for humankind because of our deep-rooted anxiety, which is part of the human condition and should not be labelled neurotic. Fear of loss and terror of extinction, he wrote, were a natural part of the human process of ageing and would not respond to any therapy. Tillich rejected the notion of a personal God – something that is traditional in Western beliefs – and of a God who kept interfering in the life of the universe, a concept shared by Western and Eastern traditions. He taught instead that a God above the personal God should be sought out via religion. He maintained that this was part of the human emotional or intellectual experience because the 'God above God' was fundamental to all emotions of courage, fear, hope and despair.

2009
Worldwide Muslim population grows to 1.57 billion

2033
2000th anniversary of death of Jesus

❝In the future we will see our religion not as supernatural doctrine, but as an experiment in selfhood.❞

Don Cupitt, 1997

It is, as yet, only a trend, and there are certainly other currents running in opposite directions. Within both Christianity and Islam, for instance, there exist a minority who feel threatened, overlooked or abused by the modern world, by its secular values, and even by its freedoms. As a result, they turn increasingly to their sacred scriptures to find reassurance and read them in an ever more literal sense, with disastrous consequences.

New perspectives The rise of intolerance should not distract attention from the real story of religion as it is lived by the many, rather than the few. New and positive perspectives have emerged in recent times, within and between the faiths. The landmark Second Vatican Council of the Catholic Church, held from 1962 to 1965, sought in the phrase of its instigator, Pope John XXIII, to 'open a window on the world'. Mutual tolerance has emerged from dialogue between churches and traditions where once there was enmity, suspicion and hostility. The gulf between the predominantly Eastern faiths and those of the West has narrowed with the demise of colonialism. Greater respect, greater knowledge and better communications have brought an interchange of ideas. Western Christians now integrate some Buddhist insights into their spiritual lives – and vice versa.

At the same time, the political pressures that sought to obliterate religion have eased. Many of the regimes, most of them Marxist, that attempted to reduce religion to just another instrument of state control have fallen, or changed course. The Chinese Communist authorities now enlist Confucius to promote landmark events such as the 2008 Olympics in Beijing. If religion has proved one thing in the last hundred years, it is that every attempt to do away with it by violence will only guarantee its survival.

Ours is often characterized as the age of religious extremism, but it is also the epoch of ecumenism and inter-faith initiatives. The first is

Numbers

It is difficult to establish the exact numbers of believers in each religious tradition because everyone uses different definitions and methods of calculation. Research published in the autumn of 2009 by the Pew Forum on Religion and Public Life in Washington DC came up with an estimate of 1.57 billion Muslims in the world, or 22.9 per cent of the global population, with 60 per cent of that number living not in Islam's traditional homeland of the Middle East and North Africa but rather in Asia. The Pew figures suggest that recent growth in numbers means that other surveys may have underestimated how many Muslims there are in the world. A digest of these other surveys puts Christians at between 30 and 33 per cent of the world population, Muslims at 18–21 per cent, Hindus at 12–15 per cent and Buddhists at 5–7 per cent. All other traditions are under one per cent.

more often reported than the second, but it is the development of dialogue, tolerance and understanding that will ultimately outflank the extremists. The actions of fundamentalists within Islam, Christianity and Hinduism in attempting to force their views on others have, everywhere they have taken place, prompted a reaction from the majority, who want to reclaim their faith and restore the true principles of religion.

The search for God The search for God, for gods, for enlightenment, for *theosis*, for Tao, for *dharma*, for Nirvana continues all around the globe among billions of people. The overwhelming majority of the world's population still choose to remain within institutional religion. Many more explore spirituality outside the conventional set-ups but are informed by the best of the faith traditions. The search may take many forms and has many names, but ultimately it is about the same thing – individuals trying through religious systems to find meaning and value in human life.

the condensed idea
Religion is in rude health

Glossary

Ahura the title of the gods worshipped by Zoroastrians

Apocalypse also known as Revelation, the last book of the New Testament, which describes a vision of the last days

atman in Hinduism the sacred power of Brahman (q.v.), which each individual experiences within him or herself

Axial Age the term used by historians to denote the period 800–300 BCE, a time of transition during which many of the world's major religions emerged

Brahman the sacred power that sustains all existing things in Hinduism; the inner meaning of existence

Brahmin a member of the priestly class in Hinduism

chi the basic energy and spirit of life in Chinese religions

dharma the truth, the way of salvation in Buddhism

diaspora the communities of Jews dispersed outside Palestine

eschatology doctrines concerning the end of history, including the coming of the Messiah, the Last Judgement and the final triumph of the faithful

fatwa a formal legal opinion or decision of a religious scholar on a matter of Islamic law

Gathas Zoroastrian scriptures

Hadith the traditions or collected maxims of the Prophet Muhammad

Hasidism a mystical movement in Judaism founded in the eighteenth century

hajj the Muslim pilgrimage to Mecca

hijrah the migration of the first Muslims from Mecca to Medina in 622 CE, an event that marks the beginning of Islam

Holy Spirit the third person of the Holy Trinity of Father, Son and Holy Spirit in Christianity

imam in mainstream Islam, the one who leads the prayers of the Muslim congregation; in Shi'a Islam it describes those descendants of the Prophet thought to enshrine divine wisdom

incarnation the embodiment of God in human form

jina one who has achieved enlightenment, a spirit, in Jainism

junzi a fully developed, wise person in Confucianism

Kabah the cube-shaped granite shrine dedicated to Allah in Mecca

Kabbalah the Jewish mystical tradition

karma action, in Buddhism, encapsulating all deeds, fears, desires and dislikes

jihad an internal effort to reform bad habits; used of late to denote a war waged in the service of religion

kenosis a Greek term used in Christianity to refer to self-emptying

Li the belief system of a *junzi* (q.v.)

mandala - a symbolic, pictoral representation of the universe in Buddhism

mantra a short prose formula or chant, originally from Vedic religions

millennium the 1,000-year period of peace and justice that some Christians believe will follow on from the end of human history, ending with the Last Judgement

moksha liberation from the cycle of birth, death and rebirth known as *samsara* (q.v.)

Nirvana denotes in Buddhism the ultimate reality, the goal and fulfilment of human life and the end of pain

Orthodox literally 'right teaching', used by Eastern Christians to distinguish themselves from Western Christians

patriarchs term originally used of Abraham, Isaac and Jacob, the ancestors of the Israelites; later of Christian leaders, especially in the Orthodox tradition

prophet one who speaks on God's behalf

rapture a Christian fundamentalist doctrine that says that the elect will be spared the 'Last Days' of Earth by being taken up to heaven to await the millennium (q.v.)

ren humanity, compassion, benevolence the chief virtue in Confucianism

Rig Veda literally 'knowledge in verse', the most sacred of the Vedic scriptures, consisting of over 1,000 hymns

samsara the cycle of birth, death and rebirth

Shahadah the Muslim proclamation of faith: 'I bear witness that there is no god but Allah and that Muhammad is his messenger'

Shar'iah 'the Path to the Watering Hole', Islamic holy law

shu the Confucian virtue of consideration, linked with the Golden Rule

Sky god the supreme deity worshipped by many people as creator of the world, eventually superseded by more immediate gods and goddesses

Sufism the mystical spirituality of Islam

Sunnah those customs sanctioned by tradition and said to imitate the behaviour and practice of the Prophet Muhammad

Talmud the classical rabbinic discussions of the ancient code of Jewish law

Torah generally used to describe the first five books of the Jewish scriptures but also used to describe laws given to Moses on Mount Sinai

Tao the way, the correct course or path, in Taoism

yoga meditative practice to eliminate egotism and achieve enlightenment

Index

Author Acknowledgements
My thanks to my editor at Quercus, Slav Todorov, and to his colleagues; to my agent Derek Johns; and to my family – Siobhan, Kit and Orla – who have listened patiently and with a convincing look of engagement as I have shared with them the details of this grand (but I hope not grandiose) tour. All biblical quotations are from the New Jerusalem Bible (Darton, Longman and Todd, 1974).

Quercus Publishing Plc
21 Bloomsbury Square
London WC1A 2NS

First published in 2010

A catalogue record of this book is available from the British Library

UK and associated territories: ISBN 978 1 84866 059 5
US and associated territories: ISBN 978 1 84866 076 2

Printed and bound in China

10 9 8 7 6 5 4 3 2 1

Prepared by Starfish Design, Editorial and Project Management Ltd